ARCHITECTURAL DIGEST
PRIVATE VIEWS

ARCHITECTURAL DIGEST
PRIVATE VIEWS
INSIDE THE WORLD'S GREATEST HOMES

EDITED BY PAIGE RENSE

ABRAMS, NEW YORK

EDITOR: Andrea Danese assisted by Laura Tam
DESIGNERS: Miko McGinty and Rita Jules
PRODUCTION MANAGER: Jules Thomson

LIBRARY OF CONGRESS CATALOGING-IN-PUBLICATION DATA
Architectural digest private views : inside the world's greatest homes / edited by Paige Rense.
   p. cm.
  Includes index.
 ISBN 13: 978-0-8109-9375-4
 ISBN 10: 0-8109-9375-9
1. Interior decoration. I. Rense, Paige. II. Architectural digest. III. Title: Private views.
NK2130.A63 2007
728—dc22

                2007015613

Printed and bound in China
10 9 8 7 6 5 4 3 2 1

HNA
harry n. abrams, inc.
a subsidiary of La Martinière Groupe
115 West 18th Street
New York, NY 10011
www.hnabooks.com

Contents

Preface

By Paige Rense

Architectural Digest's *Private Views: Inside the World's Greatest Homes* is a natural expression of our role as the international magazine of design.

Our field of focus when putting this book together was nothing less than the entire world. But how to choose from the best? For this book—as with our magazine—it's a matter of variety of tastes, locations, uniqueness, the element of discovery, the subtle and sometimes indefinable relationship a home has with its surroundings, and, as always, style.

At *Architectural Digest*, *trend* is not a concept that has a great deal of meaning. That word usually implies a predetermined equation of items, colors, and effects, as though following the right formula were the same as creating a satisfying interior design. Trends announce themselves, enjoy their tenuous hold on the spotlight, and quickly appear awkward and contrived as they fade from the scene.

We prefer to speak of *style*, which is really a way of seeing and living creatively in the world. That world is exemplified in this book by violinist Ole Bull's Moorish summer villa in Norway, Georgia O'Keeffe's Ghost Ranch in New Mexico, Catherine the Great's Chinese Palace in St. Petersburg, a couple's eight-story tower set amid Kenya's wildlife, and even a yurt, a traditional house for the nomadic people of Inner Mongolia.

The thirty homes selected here, spanning five continents, confirm our belief that great style—with its many forms, inspirations, and influences—is universal. Each of these residences illustrate the creative spark of expert design—seeing how things fit together and grasping the vital connections that others miss. The means of expression may differ, but the results always reflect imagination, self-knowledge, and authority.

The beauty of these homes speaks for itself, making our jobs as journalists easy. We do not produce or in any way set the stage—we report, conveying to the reader what talented designers and architects create and how people of taste live.

It is very much in order to acknowledge the extraordinary research and creative contributions of James Munn, special projects manager at *Architectural Digest*. Other *AD* staff members whose assistance was vital were executive editor Margaret Dunne and photographer director James Huntington, who helped in the selection process, senior editors Mary Ore and Nora Krug, contributor Kelly Sanchez, and research editor Maile Pingel. Thanks also go to the team at Harry N. Abrams, which includes editor in chief Eric Himmel, senior editor Andrea Danese, editorial assistant Laura Tam, and designers Miko McGinty and Rita Jules.

The late Coco Chanel, whose own apartment was featured in *Architectural Digest* (January/February, 1973, September 1988), once said, "Fashion passes, style remains." We do not believe that anyone has said it better. We have chosen the homes in *Private Views* to stimulate, delight, and inspire—and to display this lasting quality of style.

Many celebrated homes featured in Architectural Digest *do not appear here precisely because they* are *so celebrated, having subsequently been the subject of numerous articles and books. The following are among them: Le Corbusier's Villa Savoye near Paris; The Breakers in Newport, Rhode Island; Philip Johnson's Glass House in Connecticut; John Lautner's Sheats–Goldstein House; Thomas Jefferson's Monticello; Greene & Greene's Gamble House; and practically anything and everything by Frank Lloyd Wright.*

The Czar's Private Apartments in the Kremlin

A Rare Look at the Imperial Suite Designed for Nicholas and Alexandra in Moscow

Text by Peter Lauritzen

Photography by Jaime Ardiles-Arce and Yuri Dimitriev

Ever since 1918, when Lenin moved the capital back to Moscow from St. Petersburg, the Great Palace inside Moscow's ancient fortress, or Kremlin, has stood at the heart of Russian government. Its vast halls served as the setting for important ceremonies, just as they had done under the czars, while many of the events of Russia's tumultuous history came to a climax in formal announcements made beneath the great dome of the octagonal Saint Vladimir Hall. Both Lenin and Stalin lived within the Kremlin walls, although not in the Great Palace, and during their lifetimes and up until 1955 the entire area was closed to outsiders.

For the two hundred years before the revolution, the czars themselves resided in St. Petersburg and visited Moscow only on special occasions. The private apartments in the Great Kremlin Palace are small and intimate compared with the grand state rooms in the Winter Palace in St. Petersburg or the imperial summer residences at Peterhof or Tsarskoye Selo. Under the imperial regime, accredited visitors could obtain permission to visit any of these residences in the czar's absence, but the Kremlin apartments required a special permit not only from court officials but from the chief of the Moscow police. The apartments provided a perfectly preserved glimpse into Russia's imperial past.

Because the czars came so seldom to Moscow and the Kremlin no longer served as the fortified center of government, by the mid-eighteenth century many of its buildings had been allowed to deteriorate. Catherine the Great had a plan drawn up to raze many of the lesser structures while bringing the others together under a single roof. But it would be her grandson Nicholas I who, in ordering the construction of the Great Kremlin Palace in 1838, would finally realize her plans for sweeping

Surviving as a splendid reminder of Russia's imperial past are the private apartments of the czars in Moscow's Great Kremlin Palace. OPPOSITE: The largest of the ceremonial halls in the palace was dedicated to St. George. Six gilt-bronze chandeliers run the length of the hall.

LEFT: Built within the fortified walls of the Kremlin between 1838 and 1849, the palace was used by the czars only for official ceremonies.

changes to the historic complex on the Moskva River. In the meantime, many of the Kremlin buildings had suffered a fate worse than neglect: The cataclysmic fire that devastated Moscow in 1812 became the stuff of legend. It was said to have been set by the Muscovites themselves in a desperate attempt to prevent the occupation of their beloved city and its historic citadel by Napoleon.

In 1818, seven years before he succeeded his brother Alexander I as Autocrat of All the Russias, Nicholas and his pregnant wife, Alexandra Feodorovna, were sent to live in the fire-ravaged precinct of the Kremlin. The dowager empress had wanted her first grandchild to be born in Moscow. "This was [done]," Alexandra wrote, "to raise the spirits of the inhabitants of the old capital." The son born to Nicholas and Alexandra would eventually succeed his father as Czar Alexander II, grandfather of the last czar of Russia and the only one of Peter the Great's successors to be born in the Kremlin.

Nicholas returned to Moscow in 1825 to be crowned czar in the Uspensky Sobor, the Kremlin's Cathedral of the Assumption, but on his accession he also inherited his brother's legacy of the triumph over Napoleon in 1812. To commemorate the twenty-fifth anniversary of the victory, Nicholas had a vast church built just south of the Kremlin. Although it wasn't completed until 1883, the Church of the Savior, designed by Konstantin Andreevitch Thon, was long regarded as "the most beautiful church in Moscow." Its great gilt dome dominated the Moscow skyline until 1934, when Stalin ordered it blown up as part of the militant atheism of Soviet communism.

Only two years after work began on the church, Nicholas commissioned Thon to build the Great Kremlin Palace. Finished in 1849, the palace was distinguished by

LEFT: One of the largest rooms in the apartments, the czarina's study contains an upright piano. The furniture is embellished with Boulle marquetry, a passion of Nicholas I. The chandeliers are crystal.

BELOW AND OPPOSITE: An ormolu-mounted fireplace of malachite is the focal point of the boudoir. Since the private apartments occupied the ground floor, massive piers are visible supports for the grand ceremonial halls above. As throughout, one side of the boudoir opens to the adjacent rooms, creating a corridor along which the czar would pass.

ABOVE: Moiré silk adorns nearly every surface in the Blue Bedroom, which was used by the czar and czarina. Its restrained giltwork contrasts with the sumptuously decorated adjoining boudoir. On the Carrara marble mantel is an ormolu-mounted globe clock from France.

Thon's eclectic architectural style and boasted a 410-foot-long river façade. Its layout and plan, apart from replacing old, fire-scarred, or otherwise dilapidated buildings, was to be an expression of its imperial function.

Ancient protocol prescribed that the new sovereign first appear to the Muscovites at the top of the Red Staircase of the Palace of Facets before descending to enter the adjacent Cathedral of the Assumption for the lengthy coronation ceremony. Thon therefore planned a series of immense halls on the upper floor of the Great Kremlin Palace that would allow the czar to pass among nobles, court officials, and sundry other dignitaries before reaching the fifteenth-century Palace of Facets, which takes its name from its façade of diamond-cut granite blocks. Each of the ceremonial halls was given the name of one of Russia's orders of chivalry: the Saint Andrew Hall, for example, served as the throne room, and the Saint George Hall, illuminated by six huge

gilt-bronze chandeliers and 3,200 candles, was dedicated to the patron saint of Russia's principal military order. Just beyond lay the domed Saint Vladimir Hall, named for the first Russian ruler to convert to Christianity and the patron of an order created by Catherine the Great in 1782.

Since it was only on their coronations that the czars were expected to reside in Moscow, the private apartments designed by Thon and decorated according to Nicholas's rich but varied taste were not only quite small by czarist standards, they were situated on the ground floor of the building. In fact, they were laid out between the giant piers built by Thon to support the ceremonial halls on the floor above. The imperial suite consists of only seven rooms, sufficient for the czar and czarina alone; their immediate family and the remainder of their entourage were housed on estates outside Moscow.

Because the rooms were used so infrequently, subsequent czars never bothered to redecorate. Some 150 years after their creation, they reflect the interests of Nicholas I, who wanted his formal apartments to spotlight Russia's wealth in natural resources. Dazzling 24-karat gold-leaf detailing brightened the dull northern light of dark winter days and emphasized the size of Russia's gold reserves—the greatest known in the world at the time. Chandeliers of crystal and glass were proof of another Russian industry, while the rich mineral deposits of the Urals provided rare veined jasper, agate, lapis lazuli, and malachite, which were used for decorative veneers. Endless varieties of wood were inlaid in intricate patterns on the floors, while the doors and many of the furnishings displayed Nicholas's passion for Boulle marquetry.

BELOW: The czar's study, which is almost precisely the way Nicholas II left it, is typical of the design of studies in aristocratic Russian residences. Ash paneling and birch and cherry furnishings complement simple document cabinets finished without the ormolu or gilt that had once embellished Russian Empire pieces.

BELOW RIGHT: In the corridor-like sitting room set aside for the czarina's ladies-in-waiting, walnut carvings frame wall panels painted to look like tapestries. The woodwork and the curving backs of the chairs and settee reflect the nineteenth-century interest in elaborate ornamentation.

Each room in the apartments opened into the next, forming a long corridor that was used for splendid processions led by the czar on ceremonial occasions. The last czar, Nicholas II, came to Moscow more often than did any of his predecessors, and from these rooms he mounted the great parade staircase to preside over ceremonies that today seem full of tragic irony. The last imperial ceremony at the palace took place August 18, 1914, on the outbreak of World War I. Maurice Paléologue, the French ambassador, recorded the event:

We were ushered into the Saint George Hall, where the high dignitaries of the empire . . . were already assembled in a dense and silent throng. On the stroke of eleven o'clock the czar, the czarina, and the imperial family made their ceremonial entry. . . . In a full, firm voice the czar addressed the nobility and people of Moscow. . . . He declared that a heroic national impulse was sweeping over all Russia, without distinction of race or nationality, and concluded: 'From this place, the very heart of Russia, I send my soul's greeting to my valiant troops and my noble allies. God is with us!'

The French ambassador was then invited to join the czar's entourage through the Saint Vladimir Hall until they reached the Red Staircase. "The moment the czar appeared a storm of cheering broke out from the whole Kremlin, where an enormous crowd, bareheaded and struggling, thronged the pavement," he wrote. Paléologue's account ends with a somber reflection on all that the Kremlin had seen, wondering at the terrifying lessons that history proposes.

More than a decade after the collapse of the Soviet Union, with the opulence and turbulence of Russia's imperialist past grown increasingly distant, Paléologue's observations on Moscow's relics still resonate:

I spent the afternoon seeing Moscow, lingering particularly over the places hallowed by memories of 1812. . . . At the Kremlin the ghost of Napoleon seems to rise up at every step. From the Red Staircase [Napoleon] watched the progress of the fire during the baneful night of September 16. . . . It was there that he had that clear and pitiless vision of his impending ruin: 'All this,' he said repeatedly, 'is the herald of great disasters.'

Georgia O'Keeffe's Ghost Ranch

The Artist's First New Mexico Home Is Faithfully Restored

Text by Dana Micucci
Photography by Robert Reck

For more than forty years, Georgia O'Keeffe spent her summers at Ghost Ranch, some sixty miles northwest of Santa Fe. "I loved it immediately," she said of her first visit to New Mexico. "From then on I was always on my way back." OPPOSITE: O'Keeffe would climb the ladder to the roof, where she often slept.

BELOW: "To me it is the best place in the world," said O'Keeffe of Ghost Ranch. "It has always been secluded and solitary. When I first went there, it was only one house with one room—which had a ghost living in it."

"As soon as I saw it, I knew I must have it," said Georgia O'Keeffe of the simple adobe house at Ghost Ranch, her first residence in her beloved New Mexico. O'Keeffe first stayed at the twenty-one-thousand-acre dude ranch in 1934, having already spent several summers in northern New Mexico, captivated by the piercing sunlight, expansive skies, and stark beauty of the high-desert landscape that have long attracted artists to the region.

Here in this unpretentious, U-shaped structure, situated in a remote area of the ranch, O'Keeffe spent each summer and fall of most of the last forty years of her long and prolific life. (She died in 1986 at the age of ninety-eight.) Its adobe walls seemingly an extension of the earth itself, the Ghost Ranch house nurtured her love of nature. Its picture windows frame views of majestic cliffs and mesas. O'Keeffe expressed her enthusiasm for her surroundings in a 1942 letter to the painter Arthur Dove:

> I wish you could see what I see out the window—the earth pink and yellow cliffs to the north—the full pale moon about to go down in an early morning lavender sky . . . pink and purple hills in front and the scrubby fine dull green cedars—and a feeling of much space—It is a very beautiful world.

She immortalized the landscape around her home, in all its shifting moods and colors, in paintings such as *The Cliff Chimneys*, 1938; *Untitled (Red and Yellow Cliffs)*, 1940; and *My Front Yard, Summer,* 1941, which depicts a vista of her "private mountain," the Cerro Pedernal. "Out here, half your work is done for you," O'Keeffe said. She particularly delighted in climbing the hand-hewn wooden ladder to the roof, where she often entertained visitors and slept under the stars.

A component of the Georgia O'Keeffe Museum Research Center, which is affiliated with Santa Fe's Georgia O'Keeffe Museum, the artist's house at Ghost Ranch has been restored to its original 1940s appearance, based on photographs from the period. The ranch itself, located some sixty miles northwest of Santa Fe, now functions as an educational-conference center run by the Presbyterian Church.

At Ghost Ranch, O'Keeffe composed a life of Zen-like simplicity. The stark desert landscape corresponds to the austerity of the house and its interior as well as to her austere, self-sufficient image. O'Keeffe's minimalist aesthetic, rooted in her appreciation of Asian art and the design-driven teachings of artist Arthur Wesley Dow, with whom she studied at Columbia University in 1914–15, is evident throughout. The rooms are decorated with a careful assemblage of found objects and functional furniture and open onto a central patio, overgrown with gray-green chamisa and sagebrush. Adobe fireplaces and walls, and the viga-and-*latilla* ceilings typical of New Mexican adobe-style architecture, endow the house with a welcoming, earthy intimacy.

Though modest in appearance, it exudes a certain harmony, as if every element were in its proper place, reflecting O'Keeffe's attention to detail.

Her studio is a tranquil, whitewashed space with a hardwood floor and an adobe fireplace, above which hangs a bleached animal skull. Displayed on the mantel and windowsills, as well as on the naturally grained cedar ledge encircling the room, are gnarled branches and animal bones, reminiscent of the objects that she scavenged from the desert. The originals were donated, along with O'Keeffe's art materials and personal possessions, to the Georgia O'Keeffe Museum Research Center in Santa Fe by artist Juan Hamilton, O'Keeffe's friend and associate, and his wife, Anna Marie.

All of the artist's furnishings remain in the house, arranged as she once lived among them. In the studio, where O'Keeffe installed a picture window to maximize the desert view, are a scattering of rush-seated chairs, a

LEFT: A ledge displays bones and other objects found by the artist. "The bones seem to cut sharply to the center of something that is keenly alive on the desert even though it is vast and empty and untouchable—and knows no kindness with all its beauty," she once said.

modest wooden table, and a red canvas and chrome Le Corbusier–style lounge chair. White cotton curtains shade the windows. The artist's easel, which supports a large, primed blank canvas, stands in a corner. A small wooden bench and a metal cart bearing tin cans of paintbrushes, paint tubes, and other supplies are nearby.

The room adjacent to the studio served variously as a bedroom and a sitting room where O'Keeffe often listened to classical music. It is furnished with several rudimentary tables, a simple black chair, an old stereo, and the plain desk on which O'Keeffe penned her numerous letters to her husband, photographer and gallery owner Alfred Stieglitz, who never set foot in New Mexico.

Even sparer in appearance is the artist's corner bedroom, in which two perpendicular walls of glass offer an unobstructed view of the red-and-yellow cliffs in what she called her backyard. A flagstone floor and a modest twin bed dressed in white cotton sheets add to the monastic aura of the space. Cedar wall ledges display seashells and rocks, another reminder of O'Keeffe's love of simple natural forms.

"O'Keeffe had a profound connection to nature, its forms, shapes, and contours. Her main objective was to distill her experience of the world around her to its essence," says Barbara Buhler Lynes, curator of the Georgia O'Keeffe Museum and the Emily Fisher Landau

ABOVE: The house, with Cerro Pedernal in the distance. "I suppose I could live in a jail as long as I had a little patch of blue sky to look at," O'Keeffe said. "The kinds of things one sees in cities . . . it's better to look out the window at the sage."

director of its research center. "The solitude and raw, elemental beauty she found at Ghost Ranch brought her closer to that essence."

The dining room is minimally furnished, with a long plywood table, tall-backed Chinese chairs, and an Art Deco–style floor lamp. Polished black stones, carefully arranged on the windowsill, glisten in the sunlight. Adjacent to the dining room are the kitchen and pantry, precisely ordered with the artist's spices, canning jars, baskets, and myriad cooking utensils. O'Keeffe enjoyed eating in the vestibule off the kitchen, where she would sit on the *banco* (adobe ledge) and look out onto the New

Mexican desert, studded with wildflowers and stunted piñon and juniper trees.

The Ghost Ranch residence represented for the artist "a kind of freedom," she said, despite the hardships of living in isolation with generator-supplied electricity and without a telephone or fresh fruits and vegetables, for which she had to drive to Santa Fe on a dirt road.

Her daily routine here was marked by her reverence for simple rituals and an inner clarity that allowed her to be fully present in each moment. She would rise early and take a long walk before breakfast, accompanied by her dogs. After breakfast, she would venture back into the

OPPOSITE: Windows in the kitchen open to the high-desert landscape.

ABOVE: The studio at Ghost Ranch remained an austere space with few furnishings. O'Keeffe also painted outdoors, and her Model A Ford functioned as a kind of mobile studio. "I thought the ranch would be good for me because nothing can grow here," she said.

desert for a day of painting, often using her Model A Ford as a portable studio. Upon returning home, she would take an evening walk before dinner. The lasting impression of O'Keeffe's legendary life and art, and the Ghost Ranch home that stood at its center, is that of a woman completely at ease with the natural world and with herself.

BELOW: The Le Corbusier–style lounge chair in the studio is original to the house. Small items were given to the Georgia O'Keeffe Museum in Santa Fe by her friend and associate, Juan Hamilton. The house is now used for research activities.

OPPOSITE: As elsewhere in the house, rocks, shells, and bones collected by the artist on her walks adorn the dining room. Chinese chairs surround the plywood table. The U-shaped adobe structure was built in the 1930s; it now sits on about twelve acres.

David Bowie

The Musician's Indonesian-Style Refuge on Mustique

Architecture by Arne Hasselqvist
Interior Design by Robert J. Litwiller and Linda Garland
Landscape Design by Michael White
Text by Christopher Buckley
Photography by Derry Moore

OPPOSITE: Architect Arne Hasselqvist conceived a series of Japanese/Scandinavian pavilions on Mustique for David Bowie and his wife, Iman. Indonesian elements, including the Javanese dining pavilion, right, were introduced by Bali-based designer Linda Garland.

One of the cruising guides to the Grenadines sports a hand-drawn map of the island of Mustique that shows its various points of interest. Here is "Princess Margaret's ho." There's "Mick Jagger's ho." And up here, high on a hillside, is "David Bowie's ho." And one heck of a ho it is, five years and more than fourteen cargo containers in the making, culminating in an Indonesian-style pavilion that horseshoes around two koi-filled ponds that descend burblingly toward the setting sun into a sort of *trompe-l'eau* sluice from which dark water appears to emerge magically pristine as it pours into the swimming pool. Indonesia in the Caribbean? But of course. No architecture is out of context on Mustique, an island of follies and Taj Mahals and Kyoto gardens. "It's a whim personified," says David Bowie. "I love a good cliché, and this house for me is just the most delightful cliché."

Bowie, his mismatched eyes asparkle with intelligence, wit, mimicry, and a distinctly sexual energy, drags on the umpteenth Marlboro of the morning. He was twenty-two when he became famous with the song "Space Oddity," a soulful dirge about an alienated astronaut named Major Tom. He released it to coincide with *Apollo 11*, and when BBC-TV played it moments after Neil Armstrong planted his feet on lunar soil, Bowie too was launched. He brought to rock his own theater of the absurd with a succession of extremely dramatic personae—Major Tom, the androgynous Ziggy Stardust, Aladdin Sane, the Mephistophelian Thin White Duke.

Role changes have always been part of Bowie's persona. Born David Jones, he grew up in the London suburb of Bromley, the son of a children's home administrator. His father bought him a saxophone, and he adopted the stage name of Tom Jones—for a week, until he saw photographs of another fellow, a singer, who went by the name. He changed it back to David Jones. Then along came the pop group The Monkees, with lead singer Davy Jones. He called himself David Jay for a bit, but decided that it lacked a certain je ne sais quoi. By then

ABOVE: Bowie stands by the gilt Balinese-style living room doors.

Mick Jagger had become the flaming hot rocker. Jagger . . . dagger . . . Bowie was into Americana . . . knife . . . presto—David Bowie! The rest is anything but silence; it's been very loud indeed.

In 1990 he made the gutsy, artistic move of announcing that he would perform his greatest hits one more time on tour and then never again, in order to force himself to produce a new repertoire. Since 1992, he has been married to Iman Abdulmajid, a.k.a. Iman, the painfully beautiful (but not as tall as you thought) Somalian model and actress. But about the ho.

"Why Mustique indeed," Bowie begins. "Frankly, it was quite odd. I went down to spend a couple of days with Mick and Jerry in their house, and while waiting for the boat—I was going to take a trip up and down the Caribbean and it never happened because the propeller fell out or something—I was stranded. And I just went scouting one day, having nothing better to do, there

being little else to do there, and I came across this area of land attached to Arne Hasselqvist's. And we talked about it, and I thought, Why not?"

Colin Tennant, Lord Glenconner, bought the island for a pittance in the late '50s and cleverly developed it by planting it with a royal seed, Princess Margaret, to whom he gave a parcel of land as a wedding present. He then enlisted Swedish architect Hasselqvist to transform her uncle-in-law Oliver Messel's watercolor architectural sketches into an actual ho. Hasselqvist stayed on Mustique and to date has built roughly half of the island's houses, including his own breathtaking Japanese hilltop house, similarly arranged around tranquil koi pools.

"Arne was willing to sell," Bowie continues, "if the sister house to be built on the site matched in weight the house he'd built for himself. I could agree to that, but then what to do with it? I said to him, 'Look, you've obviously been to the East, Arne. Have you ever been to

LEFT: An octagonal guest pavilion with palm-tree trunks and an ornamental bamboo ceiling was constructed by landscape designer Michael White on Bali and reassembled on the site. A Javanese gaming table is flanked by nineteenth-century planter's chairs.

BELOW: A carved and painted detail.

OPPOSITE: "You're never able to see much of the house at one time," says interior designer Robert J. Litwiller. "We hit upon a formal European living room that enhances the whole 'British retreat in the tropics' concept." Garland, who designed the nineteenth-century-style furnishings, used antique beveled glass for the shutters. At left is a set of circa 1825 engravings of the pagodas of Pagan and Rangoon. The circa 1850 crystal oil chandelier, one of the final details of the five-year project, was found in London.

Indonesia?' He'd had a romp through there, so he knew what I was talking about. He had an idea for the waters going into the pools and into the swimming pool. And then I brought in Robert Litwiller to start constructing, in a vaguely Indonesian style, a potpourri of all the islands of Indonesia, running the whole gamut, the ring of fire." He laughs. "I wanted my own bit of the ring of fire. I wanted the sapphire," he says, the songwriter wringing out any rhyme. "I wanted something as unlike the Caribbean as possible, because it's a fantasy island, Mustique. Everybody just builds a getaway from it all so they can get there and see the same people they see all around, but in a holiday situation." A tropical hothouse version of Gatsby's East Egg, where everyone went "to be rich together."

Bowie's main residence is in Lausanne, Switzerland. He has an apartment in Los Angeles and a boat in the Mediterranean, "which I don't see enough of." He spends five or six weeks on Mustique over Christmas, and then goes back for a bit in midyear. He says he keeps things intimate, inviting just a small circle of friends, Iman, and his son, Zowie, now called Joe. "I throw one

big party a year. This year it was a New Year's party, the theme being the '70s. I put on a disco, and Iman brought a mirrored ball down with her, an electric one. We had dinner for fifty but then invited people in for dancing afterwards. They all go down to Basil's when they've had enough. That's the one bar on the island. I'm up on the hill, which keeps me away from the odd tourist boat, which is getting less and less frequent because we're being quite strict about what anchorage we'll make available, because one used to get tourists coming up in cars and people-spotting, of course, basically because of Mick, myself, and Princess Margaret's house." As for being a landmark in the cruising guide, he says, "That's Basil's advert," and does an imitation: "You may well be roobin shoulders with David Booey orr maybe Mick Jagger when you come to Basil's!" He notes, "I've not had my shoulder rubbed, yet."

Jagger, he explains, came to Mustique via Princess Margaret. "Mick had been with that crowd for quite some time. He knew them all through the '60s. The Stones were of course the house band for all the coming-out parties in the '60s. 'Let's get the Rolling Stones! Daddy, can

ABOVE: Iman on a nineteenth-century Indian recliner.

OPPOSITE: A section of the horseshoe-shaped veranda circles the upper pond. Teak housefronts from the Javanese village of Kudus were used as façades for the kitchen area. The intricately carved columns were inspired by originals on the island of Sumbawa.

we have the Rolling Stones?' 'Well, tell them to wash before they come.' That sort of thing. So he moved in those circles at a very young age." Jagger's house, like Hasselqvist's, is Japanese style, with a great croquet lawn.

So Bowie bought the land in 1986, and the house was ready, except for finishing touches, by Christmas 1989, an accomplishment that deservedly swells the chest of New York designer Litwiller, who coordinated the disparate contributions of Hasselqvist, and designer Linda Garland and landscape architect Michael White, both of whom live half-worlds away on Bali.

It was the redoubtable Litwiller who oversaw every detail, including the shipping containers from Indonesia, Italy, England, New York, and Atlanta, with their concomitant nightmare of international paperwork and customs clearances. "It was something," Litwiller says of the project with a wan smile, "I choose not to remember." It was also, he adds, an education, during which he learned, amid much else, of the ingenuity of termites, which will bore up through thick concrete, traverse underneath floor tiles, and then burrow precisely through those to get at the leg of a bamboo chair, pure candy to them. "So you have to be very careful no one heavy is sitting in it," he says. Not likely in this household. My Labrador retriever weighs more than Bowie and Iman together.

In October 1990 a mutual friend brought Bowie together with Iman. "I'd just come out of one relationship

and I was really completely uninterested in forming a new one. And then we had dinner in Los Angeles, and it was over. Or rather, it began. She'd just been there a year. She'd quit modeling to endeavor to create a new career for herself, acting, a very brave thing to do. She was very hard-line about modeling: 'That's it, I'm at the top, I'll stop.' She did *Star Wars*. Not *Star Wars*, what's that other space thing? *Star Trek*. *Star Trek 39*. And she did *House Party 2*. She did a television movie called *Lies of the Twins*, and for the first year in Hollywood, that's pretty good."

Bowie has called himself an entertainer, not a musician. "Oh yeah, absolutely. I've been lucky with the songs. I can't play anything well." This is an amusing admission from a multiplatinum rock aristocrat. "I play what is politely called 'composer's piano,' which means I know enough chords to be able to find my way around a song but not enough to sit down on stage, like Elton John, for instance, who's a wizard pianist. I'll have a go at anything and get a screech or an oink out of it, and then think, Well, that's kind of nice, play it three times and it'll sound like an arrangement." He adds, "I think that's the secret to half of my success as a composer."

Bowie has worked in almost all the arts. He's acted in movies, playing an alcoholic alien in Nicolas Roeg's *The Man Who Fell to Earth*, a vampire with Catherine Deneuve and Susan Sarandon in *The Hunger*, and a prisoner of war in *Merry Christmas, Mr. Lawrence*. He debuted on Broad-

way in 1980 in the title role in *The Elephant Man*. He's narrated *Peter and the Wolf* with Eugene Ormandy and the Philadelphia Orchestra and recorded a duet performance of "The Little Drummer Boy" with Bing Crosby. (Bowie and Der Bingle, conjure on that.) Crosby, he recalls, was by then "pretty far gone, but he had a splendid voice, very loud." He says he's been working on a screenplay "eternally," which he would like to direct. He sculpts and paints, though he never paints on Mustique because, he says, "the light frightens me. It's incredibly bright. I'm not used to working in the light. And I'm not terribly good. It shows too many flaws when you're painting in very bright light. Technique goes to hell. So I'll retain that for the murk of Berlin or somewhere."

It's time to go. He has to get on a plane, which he "loathes" so much that at the height of his touring career in the '70s, when he was on the road eleven months a year, he went an entire six years without flying, requiring some truly Phineas Fogg–like improvisations.

His house overlooking Lake Geneva is where he works and writes. But Bowie's heart seems to be in Tennant's "strange netherworld—nutty, potty" Mustique, this semi-sceptered isle, this rhinestone set in a turquoise sea, "this storehouse of anecdotes, none of which will pass my lips," he laughs. "My ambition is to make music so incredibly uncompromised that I will have absolutely no audience left whatsoever and then I'll be able to spend the entire year on the island."

BELOW: A collection of nineteenth-century Egyptian Revival furniture highlights the master bedroom. In the corner is an inlaid nineteenth-century Moroccan chest-on-stand. The floors are covered with antique lacquered rattan matting.

OPPOSITE: "The house is such a tranquil place that I have absolutely no motivation to write a thing when I'm here," says Bowie. "The first view from the entrance is of two fish ponds and the pool, beyond which is Britannia Bay, where the yacht is anchored," notes Litwiller.

ABOVE: "My great-great-grandfather Raizeman Newton Webster built the house in 1850," says John Loring. "It sits on a double lot right on the town square. Everyone in the family has always had a special affinity for the place because their childhoods were spent here on vacations. It has many mad details."

John Loring's Red House

Souvenirs of a Family Heritage in Michigan

Text by Brooks Peters
Photography by Tony Soluri

"There are very few humble American houses that have been lived in for over 140 years," says John Loring, Tiffany's design director, describing the Red House, his family's homestead in western Michigan. "It was built in 1850 by my great-great-grandparents the Websters, who moved here from Ohio. They built the entire thing themselves, by hand." Sharp-eyed shoppers might recognize the residence as the image featured on one of Tiffany's Battersea enamel boxes. Over the years it has proved to be one of the store's best-selling items.

"The Red House is popular because it represents the typical American dream," says Loring, who spent most of his childhood summers playing amid its myriad nooks and crannies. "No other country could have produced a house like it. The Red House hasn't been copied after a European prototype. Nothing has been done to impress, but everything to please. The American furnishings do not daunt you with their authority as you cross the threshold. The entire place is open wide and welcoming, with a heart as big as a public square."

"Over the years the Red House has developed a rich texture that is irreplaceable," notes Loring. BELOW: Circus owner Burr Robbins, who was Loring's great-grandfather, acquired the living room's Kirman carpet in the 1880s. The velvet-covered Eastlake-style furniture is original to the house. Lobmeyr chandelier.

Located, in fact, on the public square in a small town in Michigan's wine-growing region, the Red House has not always been so inviting. After Loring's grandmother, who maintained a primary residence in Chicago, grew too old to cope with its upkeep, she put a cyclone fence around the property and temporarily shut its doors. "It was a very unhappy state of affairs," he recalls. "The hedges were unpruned—it was not attractive. It was dismal." Then, in the early '6os, Loring's mother, China (a name that's been passed down through several generations), asked her son to look the place over and help her decide if it would be possible to restore the landmark to its prime. "I told her yes," Loring says, "so Mom took a deep breath, plunged in, and took it all apart. She stripped it right down to the tulipwood floors. She also went to everyone in the family and asked them to return whatever things they might have borrowed. Fortunately they all cooperated. And thank heavens. It would not have survived another ten years in that condition."

Nearly two years after his mother's death, Loring gave the house another makeover. "It's an unbelievable amount of work to take everything apart and put it back together again," he says with an amused sigh of exasperation. "The plasterwork, which was all original, had to be redone, and the exterior clapboards had to be taken down, repaired, or replaced. Now it looks exactly the way it did before, so no one notices. But things are no longer askew."

Though Loring visits the Red House throughout the year, shuttling back and forth between his residences in Manhattan and Paris, he makes an extra effort to spend the bulk of his summers there. Each weekend it's packed with friends and family. "Very often there are eight people in the house at the same time," he says, "eating, cooking, relaxing with a cool drink on the porch, gardening, going off on adventures, or just sitting around the living room having tea. The Red House belongs to everyone. It's like a very complex parlor game. You enter and automatically feel that you know how to play. Everything is possible."

LEFT: A table in the library displays circus memorabilia, along with a Louis Comfort Tiffany vase and lamp and a contemporary Tiffany's enamel box depicting the Red House.

If the Red House reflects the American dream, its most celebrated resident, Burr Robbins, represents a compelling variation on the stereotypical American success story. "My great-grandfather started out in Paw Paw, Michigan, with just two trained bears," Loring explains. "Bit by bit he put together a circus that traveled around the newly settled areas along the southern tip of Lake Michigan." Eventually, the troupe evolved into the largest three-ring tent circus in the country. Souvenirs of Robbins's flamboyant extravaganzas abound in the Red House: a Bengal tiger's tooth, a camel-shaped inkwell, a poster of a polar bear, spangled elephant blankets, and snapshots of clowns, acrobats, and fire-eaters. It was Robbins who gave the red façade its cheerful yellow trim, turning it into a local landmark sometimes referred to as the Circus House.

At first glance, the Red House seems like a very different world from the sophisticated circles in which Loring travels on behalf of Tiffany's. But essential to Tiffany's legendary allure, hidden within its famous light blue packaging, and glistening amid its shiny glass counters, is a similar mystique. "The circus is about making things larger than life," Loring says, "and Tiffany's is about a similar sense of event. The Red House is great in its small way because it too is an event."

Adding to that air of theatricality is the fact that the Red House is stocked with a gallimaufry of knickknacks and ephemera that only a house constructed before the Civil War could contain. Inserted into a diary are dozens of family members' hair clippings, intricately braided and carefully labeled. "I only show them to you," Loring says, "because it is so unbelievable to find these in a house today. Some of the 'friendship braids' go back to the eighteenth century." On a shelf in the library, one finds fragments from the Roman Forum that he and his brother smuggled out of Italy. "It's not politically correct,

RIGHT: A circa 1875 polar bear poster from the Burr Robbins Circus hangs against a paisley-patterned wall in a guest bedroom. "Paisley shawls embroidered with spangles and beads were used to adorn the circus elephants," explains Loring. The array of nineteenth-century Leeds mocha ware on the chest is in honor of his father, who was born in Kirkstall, near Leeds, in 1885.

"You feel very differently about a house your family has had for almost a century and a half than you do about something bought twenty-five years ago," says Loring. "It would have been shocking to perform any radical surgery on it. We simply made things more livable." RIGHT: The dining room's portrait of his great-great-grandparents was painted for their 1842 wedding.

I know," Loring explains, "but in those days we were just normal teenage pranksters." Two pieces of limestone salvaged from the Truman-era White House renovation lie across the floor, while an elaborate Queen Elizabeth I doll stands regally atop a cabinet. There are modern treasures, too: a first edition of Anita Loos's novel *Gentlemen Prefer Blondes*, which was the last book Loring's great-grandmother bought before she died in 1925.

Moving throughout the residence's various floors (for a small building it boasts an astonishing number of rooms), one comes upon the odd Louis Comfort Tiffany lamp or some extraordinary Oriental rug, but the overall effect is modest, an unostentatious jumble of odds and ends of obscure sentimental worth. "It's fascinating," Loring says, "but if you remove any object from the house it automatically loses its value. What you see around you is simply what the people who lived here liked. They were not acquisitive. The place is an accretion of their travels and adventures, and not a display of wealth. This is a prototypical Disneyland house where everything is agreeable but nothing is real. You never get tired of it. The Red House is a rest from everyday logical life."

That escape from rigid order and convention is most evident in the choice of furnishings. "The house incorporates every style you can think of," Loring says. "In the library, for example, is an Irish Chippendale table placed next to an eighteenth-century marquetry armchair beside a Louis XV country bedside table next to a 1920s upholstered chair. The addition of a Tiffany lamp is absolutely appalling, and if you were to describe it to anybody they would simply laugh and say you're mad. But it works."

Keeping the integrity of the original house for future generations occasionally has its drawbacks. "There are times when I may not be terribly fond of having ancestors staring at me from the walls," Loring admits. "I can think of much more cheerful things to look at. But it's their house, not mine. I see myself more as a curator than as an owner. People often ask me what I'm going to do with such and such, and my answer is, but it's already been done! It's going to stay put. That's where it belongs. We don't have a sense of that anymore in America. Everything is so transient in this world. It's nice to know that some things don't change."

Crow Hollow Ranch

A Designer's East Coast Farmhouse in Montana

Architectural Design by Clive Bridgwater
Interior Design by Karin Blake
Text by Verlyn Klinkenborg
Photography by David O. Marlow

"When I was growing up," says Karin Blake, "I was taught to pick every dandelion I saw. And now look at this!" She is pointing to a field full of dandelions that begins at the fence line at her Crow Hollow Ranch and climbs up into the timber beneath the peaks of the Absaroka-Beartooth Wilderness in southwestern Montana, just outside Livingston. If Blake were indeed to pick every dandelion, she would eventually work her way up from the guesthouse to the main house, which sits in a bend of Suce Creek.

On a hot summer day, Molly, a Doberman; Menashe, a young pointer; and Livingston, a broken-tailed black-and-white cat, are lying on the porch. Their air of lassi-tude is fitting, for Blake, a Los Angeles–based designer, and her husband, William Levine, have built a remarkably relaxing place. "This is the first house I've ever actually built from scratch," says Blake. "Since I come from the East Coast, what I really wanted was a farmhouse."

What Blake has done is to revise the idea of a farmhouse, in this case one whose first principle is the porch. "I changed what in my opinion would be an East Coast farmhouse into a West Coast farmhouse with just a few little touches—I did everything on a larger scale." The deep porch has grown to heroic proportions and is now a place for dining and entertaining in summer. Inside a

LEFT: The kitchen's red pantry doors by the Wolf stove were saved from Dinah Shore and George Montgomery's California farm. Wood salvaged from buildings on the property was used for the countertops and cabinet drawers.

ABOVE: "Tucked into the end of a narrow valley and set against a national wilderness" is how Karin Blake decribes her Montana ranch. "I wanted a combination barn/farmhouse," says Blake. "The peak roof was added for a western feel." The designer brought in nineteenth-century beams and flooring to avoid a "new farmhouse look."

RIGHT: "I love the site," says Blake. "A creek wraps around the house. There are a lot of trees, which is unusual for Montana—it's more like New England. And there are great wilderness trails for riding." Adirondack chairs line the deep porch, where Blake and her husband entertain in the summer.

conventional farmhouse, it's all too common to find a warren of dark, small rooms. Not here. From the porch into the great room and from the great room into the kitchen, there is an expansive sense of flow, an ease of transition, that is rarely found in traditional farmhouses.

The effect of Blake's design is to create a weathered informality, even though the house is only fourteen years old. An enormous fireplace in the great room was built from Idaho granite. "I grew up in Bucks County, Pennsylvania," says Blake, "and so this is a bit of a carryover. I've always wanted a huge fireplace." The great room is framed with beams brought from New Hampshire, and the house has floors of wide New England boards that have already endured many generations of foot traffic. Several of the interior doors were taken from what Blake calls "a California version of an East Coast farmhouse" built in Encino by George Montgomery, the actor who was mar-

ried to Dinah Shore and was well known as a furniture maker. Set within plastered walls, the doors appear to be framed, their hues echoed by the flooring and by the varied objects of folk art that Blake has gathered around her.

What makes the farmhouse still more striking is how it steadfastly resists the clichés of modern western design. There are no horse-collar mirrors, no antler chandeliers. There are no varnished log walls or cowhide sofas. Instead, there is a strong sense of the interconnections between one place and another in Blake's life. "I had an old farmhouse on Martha's Vineyard that was my love," she says, and she has somehow yoked those places together in a way that is not an imposition on Montana.

Blake made this happen, in part, by her careful choice of site. "One of the things about the house that I love is having this creek, or 'crick,' as they say here. I think, too, because of New England, this was familiar to me." Suce

OPPOSITE: A circa 1885 wood horse and a 1920 fish decoy rest on a table in the upstairs study, which leads to the master bedroom. "I think dark woods and old leather work well here," Blake says.

BELOW: "I liked the idea of one huge room that functions for many purposes," says Blake of the great room, which runs the length of the first floor. "I followed my instincts about what pieces belonged here—I wanted to convey the spirit of the old West."

Creek curves around a corner of the house, only a few feet away from the porch. The pines that grow along its bank seem to enfold the house, and so does the enveloping sound of the water. "The guest bedroom is the best room in the house," Blake says, "because from every window you hear the creek at night."

The site was not without its problems, though. During excavation the contractor, Jim Handl, found a spring where the foundation was meant to go. But Blake insisted on her creekside location. There are now French drains beneath the house that escort the spring's outflow into the creek. The ability to overcome obstacles like that as well as Handl's superb execution of Blake's intentions—is one of the reasons Blake is so full of praise for her contractor, with whom she conferred by phone from Los Angeles in between flying in every weekend, using her husband as interpreter.

In a sense, Blake's house and its site help control the openness of the Montana landscape. The temptation, for some, might have been to build a plush, overstuffed house that wards off the outdoors. But that was not Blake's temptation. Her sense of design is based on the virtues found in the folk art she collects: simplicity, plainness, and modesty of purpose without any sacrifice of aesthetic sophistication. There are bare walls and bare floors, yet, Blake says, "this is cluttered for me." Instead of a house whose fullness banishes the outdoors, there is room for the outdoors to enter, especially in summer, when the doors to the porch are open and Menashe, Molly, and Livingston come and go at will.

ABOVE LEFT: The guest bedroom porch.

LEFT: A late-nineteenth-century log-cabin quilt and circa 1920 hickory chairs woven at the Indiana state prison are in the dining area. "I found the chairs on the East Coast, but I'm two short," says Blake.

OPPOSITE: A circa 1820 New England bench-table with its original paint occupies the master bath. The sink is vintage.

New Life for the Château du Marais

A Designer Awakens a Late-Seventeenth-Century Apartment Near Paris

Interior Design by Juan Pablo Molyneux
Text by Judith Thurman
Photography by Marina Faust

A few short years ago Juan Pablo Molyneux and his wife, Pilar, were invited by the Comte de Pourtalès—a descendant of Talleyrand's—to lease an apartment on the grounds of his estate, the Château du Marais. The word *apartment* is somewhat misleading, conjuring some drafty pied-à-terre with dubious plumbing tucked under a mansard roof. The Molyneuxs' rental, however, redefines the category. It is a classically proportioned, three-story house built in the late seventeenth century. The couple are avid bikers, and they can ride one of their vintage Harleys straight into the cobbled carriage entrance. Guests arrive with somewhat more pomp in the *cour d'honneur*. Those who stay the night have the pleasure of sleeping in a romantic *lit d'alcove* strewn with chintz roses and nestled under the beams, or a spacious bower upholstered in blue-and-white toile and furnished with iron campaign beds. Beneath the two bedroom floors are a long entrance gallery opulently hung with pumice-colored suede and scarlet damask, and a *grand salon* whose French doors lead to the terrace. Its walls of weathered stone are the embankment of a moat, and beyond it lie a hundred acres of park and lawns; a famous *miroir d'eau* (the largest such reflecting pool after Versailles); and formal gardens laid out by Achille Duchêne—the landscape architect of Blenheim Palace.

Designer Juan Pablo Molyneux renovated the apartment he and his wife, Pilar, maintain in the Château du Marais.

LEFT: The couple's wing of the palace—the portion situated in the rear corner of the L-shaped complex—dates to the late seventeenth century and comprises three stories.

The count was pleased (both as an aesthete and a land-lord) to let Molyneux refurbish the space according to his own taste, reckoning, perhaps, that the results—richly finished, consummately refined rooms—would pass muster with the château's discerning ghosts. The Marais is widely considered the most beautiful example of eighteenth-century palace architecture in private hands. Chateaubriand signed its guest book, and so did de Gaulle. It was built by Jean Benoît Vincent Barré in 1778 for Louis XVI's treasurer of the artillery—the royal defense contractor, in other words. "Teardowns are not a modern phenomenon," Molyneux says with a smile. "Barré's patron wanted a showplace, so he razed a slightly older and smaller house in perfect condition for which he had paid a king's ransom." The "new" château came into the Pourtalès family at the last fin de siècle, when the count's grandmother, née Anna Gould—a daughter of the robber baron Jay Gould—bought it as a wedding present for her first husband, Boni

de Castellane. (Her marital history is the stuff of a Henry James novel: a staggering dowry traded for an ancient title, and a feisty American heiress who finds her sea legs in the swell of a decadent society.)

Fortunes, however, tend to diminish as their heirs multiply. Succeeding generations of the family chose to share the château with select friends. "There has always been an immense waiting list for the apartments," Molyneux says, "and, of course, they never come on the market. Pilar and I first heard about the Marais as newlyweds in Argentina. Some thirty years later, when we were lunching there with the count, he happened to mention that his sister was vacating the apartment. He asked my advice on remodeling it for a new tenant, so between the main course and the dessert, we slipped away for a quick house tour. The minute I saw the terrace, I knew it had to be mine. And by the time we returned to the table, I was the new tenant."

ABOVE: An eighteenth-century giltwood chandelier lights an eighteenth-century oil, *Les Baigneuses*, and, in the foreground, a Louis XVI gilt armchair and a Régence ebony-and-bronze *bureau plat*.

OPPOSITE: The dining room has stone flooring, Italian marquetry tables, and Louis XVI chairs by Georges Jacob. Iron-and-glass lanterns hang from a ceiling dressed, like the walls, in a striped fabric.

The count's offer came at an opportune moment. Molyneux and his wife had recently sold a well-loved farm in upstate New York, two hours from their town house in Manhattan. "We are never without a country place," he says, "and we were looking for our next one. It isn't so much that we need an escape—I never seem able to leave my work behind—but Pilar and I are both nomads, so changing our setting is a form of relaxation. Even though I never feel more American than I do in France, Paris is our second home, and my office there is a base for my European projects. So it felt logical to look for something within commuting range. The Marais is thirty miles south of the city, and I think I love the getting there as much as I love the being there. Driving always clears my head."

Between his travels and commitments on several continents, Molyneux somehow found the time for an ambitious renovation. "The space had been carved into two flats," he explains, "so I knocked down their dividing walls. This added an alcove to the master bedroom and gave us an immense living room that runs the length of the ground floor. Its seating areas are defined by the three ceiling bays, and I had some fun with them. They are finished to resemble the gilt-embossed red morocco of an old book, in part because we use the room not only as a salon but as a library." The palace decorators of the seventeenth century were, like Molyneux, fond of playful trompe l'oeil, so in that spirit, he repainted the paneling to look as it might have when the house was built.

"It's a naïve, Arte Povera wall treatment—a *faux-marbre* with no pretense to realism. But exaggeration often captures an essence that fidelity doesn't—in this case, of the stone's exuberant veining and color."

Understatement is rarely the hallmark of a Molyneux interior, but a virtuoso adapts his style to any constraint. The couple's contract with the count stipulated exclusive access to a stone bridge over the moat that connects their apartment to the main château. Its upper tier is an open walkway, and beneath it runs a glass arcade with half-moon windows that was once a service passage. Molyneux had the genial idea to make this luminous sliver of space his dining room. To conceal an old heating duct, he tented the ceiling in a pale stripe. But discovering that prosaic secret does nothing to spoil the poetry of the décor: ivory-lacquered dining chairs by Georges Jacob, table settings of white majolica and Flemish glass, and flickering iron-and-glass lanterns. "It's my favorite room," Molyneux says, "and I often work here, alone, inspired by the play of light. With water on both sides and flowing beneath you, it's a good place to dream."

Love and war were plotted at the Marais, and if you have ever been on an apartment waiting list that never budges, you may consider both, in the balance, fairer than real estate. Occasionally, though, there is some poetic justice. It seems fitting that an architect and designer who has spent his career fulfilling clients' dreams of *la vie du château* should finally get a lease on his own version of it.

LEFT: The persuasiveness of Molyneux's design is due to its layering of flourishes, as in one corner of the salon. A table has a *sang de boeuf* vase mounted as a lamp and a selection of terra-cotta miniatures. The bronze ducks are eighteenth-century Persian.

Molyneux has a particular affinity for Louis XVI furnishings. "There is a masculine purity of line—straight legs, square angles—that hints at the Empire to come," he says. OPPOSITE: In the master bedroom, the lacquered armchairs, left and right; bed; and japanned commode are Louis XVI.

Sculptural Fantasy

Casapueblo—An Artist's Creation
in Uruguay

Text by Alma Jones Waterhouse
Photography by Jaime Ardiles-Arce

On the Uruguayan cliffs of Punta Ballena, where sunlight and moonlight stage a continuing theatrical performance, a castle of illusions rises on a cliff above the
ocean. It is the ever-evolving home of artist Carlos Páez
Vilaró. Hypnotic in its undulating sculptured forms of
white stucco, Casapueblo, meaning "House Village," is
Páez Vilaró's homage to life.

Impelled by the desire to create a dwelling that could
continue to grow with each life experience, the artist
responded to the untamed cliffs of this rugged promontory. "In 1960 I set up a stove on the top of the cliff and
with the help of native fishermen began building to the
beat of local tangos. We worked like the *hornero*, a
Uruguayan bird that builds a mud nest similar to a beehive, without rules or building codes.

"Casapueblo is a whole form divided into living
spaces. It is what I call 'open intimacy,' divided in a way
that gives complete independence without isolation."
His family shares this fantasia with their many guests,
who often lose themselves in the maze of passages on
the way to private concerts, festivals, and spellbinding
evenings by the ocean.

RIGHT: "In a way, my home is
a living creature that determines its own shape and
contents," says artist Carlos
Páez Vilaró of Casapueblo,
the residence he built for his
family on the cliffs of Punta
Ballena, in Uruguay. He
attributes the inspiration for
his architectural style to the
hornero, a Uruguayan bird
that "builds a mud nest similar to a beehive, without
rules or building codes."

OPPOSITE AND ABOVE:
Towerlike forms seem to grow organically from the topmost level of the house. The stuccoed form on the tiled patio—adjacent to the swimming pool—is a sculptural seating area used for sunbathing and stargazing. Near it is a small crescent-topped tower called the Half Moon Totem. On the level below is the gallery where Páez Vilaró exhibits his artworks. Guest quarters occupy the lowest level, from which stairs descend to the sea.

In his home, as in his life, Páez Vilaró delights in the unexpected and the element of surprise. "I do not think in terms of architectural style. My home has evolved from feelings, moods, and influences—Moroccan, Turkish, Indian, Polynesian, Mexican, Egyptian, and native cultures everywhere. Architecture should be felt. That's why the human element is always the heart of it."

The almost monastic simplicity of Casapueblo is dramatized by oddly shaped terraces, intriguing arcades, rounded balconies, asymmetrical arches, and winding corridors that lead to sudden confrontations with ethnic art. Startling rooftop sculptures stand like silent sentinels in a mystical world of turrets and towers.

"To obtain the right to create without architectural plans, I promised to provide the Uruguayan authorities with the designs, upon completion of the work. I told them that I was not building a house, but a sculpture big enough to let me live inside. No one would demand plans in advance for a sculpture," he says. "And I worked like a potter, using my hands to give the walls the effect of an unpolished ceramic. I wanted my home to be a lived-in sculpture—a ceramic that would hold my life, my art."

In Páez Vilaró's home, which includes twenty-four living areas and additional sleeping spaces, there are no straight lines. "Why should there be?" he asks. "The human body has no straight lines." Sinuous passageways provide access to curved alcoves and siesta nooks that invite peace. Ceilings meld into walls that slouch comfortably, with insets of sloping shelves to keep books always within reach. The home relaxes, at ease with itself.

Art is not an addition to his home. It is the home. Art and architecture are inseparable, with paintings,

OPPOSITE: A canopy of bamboo canes shades a terrace in the Green Ray Tower, named, the artist explains, for "the strange and rare phenomenon that appears like a green flash of lightning as the sun goes down into the sea." Here, as elsewhere in the residence, seating is built into the whitewashed stucco structure.

RIGHT: Within the labyrinthine reaches of the home, even a stairway has a sculptural character.

OPPOSITE LEFT: African sculpture and ethnic artifacts are an integral part of Casapueblo, as in this sitting room generously punctuated by free-form niches.

OPPOSITE RIGHT: A large arch spans the studio/gallery, where Páez Vilaró's paintings are displayed. "I think of each archway as a perpetual yawn," he says. At left is a Brazilian tapestry.

engravings, sculptures, tapestries, murals, tiles, and ceramics an integral part of every area. Indeed, Páez Vilaró's own prodigious works of art in all these mediums have been exhibited on five continents.

For an artist whose adventurous spirit seeks uncharted realms, the home must be as unconfined as light itself. "Originally I did not want windows and doors—just openings, but now Casapueblo has eighty-five windows and eighty-one doors—all salvaged from old buildings." Their history adds special meaning for the artist. "If they had been ordered preconstructed, they would have been cold. But these windows and doors have seen much life."

"In a way, my home is a living creature that determines its own shape and contents," observes Páez Vilaró. Stucco furniture seems to grow from the walls, making the interior design as integrated as a coral reef. By day, prismatic colors shimmer through sunlit interiors. By night, cones of electrical lighting merge with candlelight, while spotlights play upon the ocean.

The metamorphosis of Casapueblo has been an extraordinary experience for the artist. "I am the type of man who creates by impulse, in an hour or in an instant. When I do a painting, I never stop until I finish, but this home can never be finished, because it reflects my own

ABOVE AND OPPOSITE: Twilight accentuates the form of Casapueblo, casting shadows, emphasizing mass and void. Says the artist, "My home has evolved from feelings, moods, and influences—Moroccan, Turkish, Indian, Polynesian, Mexican, Egyptian, and native cultures everywhere. That's why the human element is always the heart of it."

searchings and the transformation of my ideas. Areas are born and changed as needed."

Like his acrylics on canvas, with their striking colors, whimsicality, and animation, Páez Vilaró's home reflects the artist's many moods. At one moment he can touch off a storm of housecleaning, which he calls "a ballet of brooms," before entertaining friends at supper with mussels and kelp fresh from the sea. At other times he keeps company with the stars in solitude. "Here I look into the sea, but I see into myself," he says. At Casapueblo, he has achieved the ultimate triumph, creating a home that allows a sense of wonder to prevail.

Changing Seasons in Kyoto

Tea Master John McGee's Historic Seventeenth-Century Farmhouse in Japan

Text by Carol Lutfy

Photography by Jaime Ardiles-Arce

John McGee's farmhouse in Koshihata on the northern outskirts of Kyoto is the oldest known residential building in a city revered for its time-honored architecture. Built for an exiled samurai and his family in 1657, the thatched and tile-roofed one-story structure upholds the architectural traditions of Japan's ancient capital with a subtle Western flair. He has infused the house with personal style while preserving its simple, peaceful atmosphere.

Idyllic is the first word that comes to mind in describing the country residence where McGee, a tea master of the Urasenke School, has lived for the past seven years. Ensconced in a bucolic setting amid rice paddies and fields of wildflowers, it commands a dramatic view of the region's breathtaking mountains.

How McGee became a tea master is as much a story of diligent training and intuitive respect for traditional Japanese aesthetics as of old-fashioned Western assertiveness. He first came to Japan in 1970 as one of twenty-five Canadians selected to work at the Osaka World's Fair. "It was a time when most Westerners were obsessed with how modern Japan had become," he remembers. "But I found myself taking daily refuge at a traditional teahouse in a nearby Japanese garden."

About a year later he heard that the Urasenke School of Tea—the largest in Japan, with almost two million followers—was willing to take on foreign students. Not realizing that the grand tea master, Soshitsu Sen XV, is considered an emperor of sorts, he brazenly showed up at his house one morning to announce his interest in studying. "He met with me," McGee says, adding with a thunderous laugh, "Of course, I expected he would." He started his tutelage under him the next day and eventually

The Kyoto house of Canadian-born John McGee, a tea master of the Urasenke School, combines traditional Japanese architecture and aesthetic sensibilities with Western-style comforts. OPPOSITE: The oldest known residential building in the city, the structure was built by an exiled samurai family in 1657.

LEFT: A view of the garden facing south from the living room takes in the thatched roof of the gatehouse, the bamboo *kenninjigaki*-style fence and the weathered-cedar veranda. "The reed sliding door, which replaces the opaque shoji that I use in the winter, allows breezes to cool the interior while also providing shade," says McGee.

became his personal attaché. Among the hundreds of tea ceremonies they have hosted together over the years are intimate gatherings for Queen Elizabeth at Katsura Villa and for former Czechoslovakian president Václav Havel at Prague Castle.

The Japanese tea ceremony, which was developed in the sixteenth century by Sen no Rikyu, is a ritualized form of making and consuming a frothy green tea that embraces an appreciation for art, architecture, pottery, flowers, and gardens. Its philosophy has shaped McGee's approach to his Koshihata farmhouse through its insistence on savoring the changing of the seasons.

From a Western viewpoint, seasons are a straightforward quarterly occurrence, but in Japan, the slight differences within seasons—between early, mid-, and late spring, for example—are equally prized and observed with a watchful eye. Furnishings, ceramics, and flowers are all rotated to reflect these subtle changes. The result is an interior that is in a constant state of flux.

After twenty-two years in Japan, McGee has assembled a superb collection of Asian sculpture, antiques, and crafts that facilitates these ongoing transformations.

Every summer he replaces the sliding shoji screens with *yoshido*, or reed blinds, in order to encourage a sense of lightness and the flow of air. He also changes the *fusuma*, or sliding doors, regularly, with his choices ranging from a set decorated with sensitive eighteenth-century ink paintings of seven sages to cheerful, contemporary images of the four seasons by Clifton Karhu, a Kyoto-based American artist.

Scrolls in the house's two *tokonoma*, or decorative alcoves, are selected to coincide with Japanese festivals and holidays. A pair of delicate sixteenth-century Chinese ink paintings of carp (propitious symbols for boys), for instance, are inevitably up around Boy's Day Festival in May. McGee also displays *waku* and haiku poetry and paintings. "These sometimes are so specific," he says, "that they can refer to the chirp of a cricket that you hear during a given week." The house is always bursting with imaginative flower arrangements that further underline the interior's seasonal character.

McGee got his start as a collector at auctions and "junk shops" in rural Japan. He still owns the first object he ever bought, a Buddha statue small enough to take

BELOW: "The *irori-no-ma* is the fireplace room," says McGee. "Like the Western fireplace, the Japanese *irori* functioned as a source of heat and a hearth where family and guests gathered, as well as a place for cooking. The gourds around it were a gift from Elsa Peretti. In its center is a teakettle I use that dates from 1598."

ABOVE: In the sitting room is a pair of ink paintings created during the late Muromachi period of the sixteenth century. "Because carp struggle against the current as they swim, they are considered symbols of perseverance. The bamboo flower container is by Fukensai, the ninth-generation grand tea master of Urasenke."

ABOVE: "The earthen-floored *genkan*, or entrance hall, is where guests remove their shoes before coming in," explains McGee. "An antique wood dog guards it. The large paper-and-bamboo lantern was made by one of the last remaining craftsmen in Saga, which is the area that surrounds the house."

with him anywhere. Though some of his finest pieces are from Japan—an awe-inspiring sculpture of the god of lightning from the Fujiwara period among them—his voracious appetite for the new gradually led him to the far corners of Southeast Asia.

Although McGee maintains a city residence a stone's throw from the Silver Pavilion in Kyoto, he was eager to find a place in the country suitable for his collection. He had his eye on the Koshihata house for eighteen years and lobbied for twelve years before he was finally able to move in. Two years later, in 1987, government officials asked him for permission to survey the structure. Equipped with X-ray cameras, they were able to ascertain that it was constructed in 1657. The site has since

been designated an Important Cultural Property in the city of Kyoto.

The house was originally the dwelling of the Kawahara family, high-ranking retainers of the influential Toyotomi clan that ruled Japan from 1582 to 1615. After the Toyotomis lost power and Osaka Castle fell in 1615, the family, which had lived in the castle compound for generations, was exiled to Kyoto.

They were apparently Johnny-come-latelies in a part of the city that dates back to the ninth century and that still bears evidence, in the remains of hefty stone foundations, of numerous samurai residences. Though it was modest by samurai standards, the structure includes a *kininguchi*, or separate entranceway, to receive nobility, which sets it

apart from traditional farmhouses. The crosspieces on the thatched gate's roof are also symbols of status.

The interior possesses several architectural elements that suggest the Kawaharas' noble roots as well. Half of the structure adheres to Shoin-style architecture, reserved at that time for the warrior class. The master of the house would customarily receive guests in the front room, or *shoin-no-ma*, while the interior spaces were combined living/sleeping quarters that were set aside for family and intimate friends. Characterized by their small size, low ceilings, and tatami-matted floors, these modest and refined rooms contrast brilliantly with the more relaxed, rural aspect of the house.

When McGee moved in, the farmhouselike part of the interior still had its original earthen floor. "By covering it with an oak floor, I was able to bring it into the design," he says. He also installed track lighting and found a silversmith's table, based on the original that Georg Jensen used in his studio, that would complement the curved wooden beams and quarter-moon-shaped *kamado*, or traditional Japanese stove, that dominates the room. Remarkable for its seamless blending of styles, cultures, and eras, the room sets the aesthetic tone for the house.

It is the slightly raised hearth area situated at the center of McGee's residence, however, that gives the entire structure a sense of continuity. The room's twenty-foot-

ABOVE: "The sunken living room flows to the kitchen just beyond the bamboo screens," says McGee. To the right stands the original *kamado*, or kitchen stove. In the foreground is a replica of a silversmith's table from the Georg Jensen workshop. "Its curves echo the crescent-moon shape of the stove." Hanging at top left is a painting by Peruvian artist Rhony Alhalel. To its right is a Burmese embroidery.

high beam ceiling and sparse furnishings serve to link the rustic with the elegant throughout the house.

These alternating moods in the interior are echoed in the many gardens that surround the house with a protective wall of greenery. Each garden surprises the visitor with an unexpected jewel, be it a wisteria trellis or a prized 350-year-old sasanqua tree (a member of the camellia family and the oldest one still living in Kyoto).

The prize among them, however, is the courtyard garden. McGee commissioned Marc Peter Keane, a Kyoto-based American landscape architect, to redesign the space, which was overgrown with weeds when he moved in. Keane uprooted them all, leaving a single bent maple as the centerpiece. His use of traditional materials—clay

tiles, moss, and stones—pays homage to the house's venerable history. "But there is a self-consciousness about the garden that is contemporary," Keane says.

"I wanted to build a contemplative garden, so I borrowed from the sea, which has always been a contemplative place for me," he adds. "The simple spiral of the moss and the rising and falling of the gravel are meant to evoke a subtle wavelike motion."

In the evenings the garden serves as a scenic setting for moon viewing, and it is an ideal spot for meditation during the day. "In Japan, everything has a front and a back, but what I like about this garden is that it is appealing from whatever angle you look at it," McGee says.

The same is unmistakably true of McGee's house.

Wyntoon

Revisiting a Northern California Refuge for William Randolph Hearst

Architecture by Julia Morgan
Text by Sally Woodbridge
Photography by Tim Street-Porter

OPPOSITE: In the 1930s, architect Julia Morgan designed several houses as part of William Randolph Hearst's Northern California retreat, Wyntoon.

William Randolph Hearst's Bavarian village on the McCloud River in Northern California is as unknown as his castle at San Simeon is famous. A state historical monument since 1958, the castle is toured by nearly a million people every year. By contrast, Wyntoon, the Bavarian estate, is a family enclave open only to the invited.

The geographic settings of the two also differ. The castle, with its crown of palms, shimmers like a mirage on the coastal mountain range. Wyntoon lies deep in an alpine forest beside a rushing river. Its fairy-tale appearance casts a spell right out of the world of Hans Christian Andersen and the Brothers Grimm.

The flamboyant, make-believe imagery of these complementary estates entirely suited their owner. Hearst's fame initially lay in his image as a newspaper magnate. But the fortune made in mining by his father, George Hearst, fueled an acquisitive nature not limited to the business world. William Randolph Hearst brought the same passion to collecting works of art as he did to buying newspapers, and architecture soon became an extension of his enthusiasm. He tinkered endlessly with the architectural settings of the historic fragments he brought from Europe. His building projects, like his journalism, were the stuff of legends.

Hearst's lordly attitude toward his houses was tempered by the great respect he held for his architect, Julia Morgan. Though Morgan was diminutive and self-effacing in dress and demeanor, her zeal for her profession matched, even surpassed, Hearst's. Architecture was her life.

Those who know Morgan's buildings have commented on the discrepancy between her work for Hearst and for other clients. For the latter, she generally designed structures that took their place modestly in their context—background buildings. For Hearst, she appeared to be a set designer—forced against her better judgment, some said, to carry out grand schemes with Hollywood overtones. Since, contrary to assumption, Morgan did not get rich working for Hearst, what led her to compromise her standards of taste?

That the relationship was important to both was clear to their associates. Morgan was the only person on earth for whom Hearst would interrupt a business meeting. For her part, no request from Hearst, however unreasonable, went unheeded. Morgan not only designed and redesigned buildings to suit his changing ideas, she also recruited and supervised the small army of craftsmen who executed the wood carvings, ceramic tiles, plaster, and ironwork that enriched the buildings. The level of

BELOW AND BELOW RIGHT:
Willy Pogany, a Hollywood set designer and illustrator of children's books, created the murals on the timber façade of Bear House, where Hearst always stayed.

LEFT: An elaborate tracery frieze and a *Lüsterweibchen* highlight an attic bedroom on the third floor of Cinderella House. A ceramic stove is at right.

craftsmanship made it possible to integrate works of art from many different periods and places.

For Morgan, who admired the medieval architect's role as an intermediary between clients and artisans, the opportunity to play that role doubtless brought great satisfaction. It was also rewarding to work for a client who had a keen sense of scale and proportion, to say nothing of the financial means to try out ideas.

While the San Simeon castle was built at the peak of Hearst's power and wealth in the 1920s, Wyntoon was begun in the early 1930s in the abyss of the Great Depression. By the late 1930s Wyntoon became a casualty of the Depression and of Hearst's chronic extravagance. The last building, Sleeping Beauty House, was left a shell, with tools, benches, and ladders its only furnishings.

In fact, Wyntoon might never have been started had not Hearst's mother, Phoebe Apperson Hearst, built a Wagnerian Gothic castle in 1902–3, downriver from where the Bavarian village later stood. Bernard Maybeck, whose protégé Morgan had been, designed the earlier building, christened Wyntoon. Made of wood and stone, it burned down around 1930. Hearst planned a new castle—his mother had died in 1919—as a collaboration between Maybeck and Morgan, but it was never built.

Meanwhile, in 1931, Morgan toured Europe in a chauffeur-driven car provided by Hearst. In Germany she sketched the colorful villages, with their picturesque half-timbered buildings that often had folkloric murals painted on the walls. Since German pine forests recalled those of California's Siskiyou County, it seemed appropriate to re-create the whole scene there.

A clearing in the forest was chosen for the village green. A fountain and other statuary from Hearst's collection were set on the greensward encircled by a loop

OPPOSITE: The Bend, remodeled by Morgan in the Gothic style, has a dining room with a vaulted ceiling.

LEFT: Hearst decorated the library at The Bend with furnishings he collected on his European travels. A decorative arch accents the Gothic door surround at rear.

BELOW LEFT: A stone fireplace warms a sitting room in Cinderella House.

BELOW: In 1934, Hearst added the rustic stone lodge called The Bend.

drive. Three buildings—Cinderella House, Bear House, and Sleeping Beauty (now Angel) House—were spaced along one side of the drive, with their backs to the McCloud River. They had steep roofs and sharply peaked gables; the forms themselves conjured up story-book scenes.

The buildings' names came from the murals painted on their exteriors by Willy Pogany, a Hungarian-born artist who came to the States in 1914. Pogany had a long and successful career as a mural painter and an illustrator of magazines and children's books (he did more than 150). As an art director of Hollywood films during the 1930s, he designed sets for United Artists, Universal, and Twentieth Century Fox. He would have been known to Marion Davies, Hearst's longtime companion, whose screen career Hearst sponsored by backing many films in which she starred. What Pogany did at Wyntoon was a combination of fairy-tale book illustration and set design.

In 1934, while work was in progress, Charles S. Wheeler—Phoebe Hearst's lawyer, who had originally owned all of the property—offered the remainder of his fifty-thousand-acre tract to Hearst. Though he could ill afford it at the time, Hearst could not resist the offer, and so Wheeler's rustic stone lodge became part of Wyntoon. The Bend, so called because it sat in a bend of the river and was horseshoe-shaped, was far too simple for Hearst's taste. Nor was it suited to his style of hospitality. Once again he called on Morgan—to do a major remodeling of the building, in a more Gothic style. But no Gothic hall, however baronial, ever provided such comfortable quarters for sleeping and bathing.

This attention to physical comfort is one of the memorable aspects of both San Simeon and Wyntoon. Homey touches—comfortable armchairs with footstools and reading lamps, writing desks, baths with river and forest views—mitigate the museumlike atmosphere. Morgan's planning also provided guest quarters with privacy and every convenience. For these and other reasons, Wyntoon remains very much a family place, a summer home that continues to serve generations of Hearsts.

RIGHT: Religious artifacts and antiques surround the mantel in one room of Bear House. The silver-gilt processional cross, at right, is near a tenth-century Italian chair.

Ohio Organic

Dynamic, Flowing Spaces Define a House Outside Columbus

Architecture by Bart Prince
Text by Michael Webb
Photography by Scott Frances

Bart Prince has described his houses as butterflies alighting in the landscape—as much a part of nature as trees and rocks, but soaring free of conventional restraints and familiar forms. In his hands wood, glass, and stone are no longer inanimate building materials but take on a life of their own. In the residence Prince designed for Steve Skilken, a Columbus, Ohio–based real estate developer, faceted glass domes that evoke a conservatory emerge from curved copper roofs and rough masonry walls, and a broad red umbrella shelters the motor court. If the house were not hidden from the highway, it would cause traffic pileups.

Skilken describes himself as an unpretentious farm boy, and, though he pilots his own helicopter between job sites, he opted to live in a modest one thousand-square-foot cabin in the woods until he was ready to commission a house. For about nine years he clipped magazine articles, saving pictures of houses he liked, but he remained noncommittal. Then he saw a feature on the residence Prince designed for Joe and Etsuko Price in southern California and immediately flew out to meet the architect and see the Price house. "I thought it was spectacular, and though Bart showed me some other

LEFT: Albuquerque, New Mexico, architect Bart Prince wanted "a sense of excitement" in the house that he designed for Steve Skilken in Columbus, Ohio. The curvilinear glass-and-copper-clad residence "had to be beautiful from the air, since Steve comes in by helicopter."

work, I had already decided he was the right choice," Skilken recalls.

Initially, the client requested a close copy of the Price house, but Prince had no interest in repeating himself. Besides, the program and the site were radically different from those of the earlier residence, which occupies an oceanfront lot and comprises a succession of inward-looking spaces containing light-sensitive Japanese art.

Skilken instead wanted an open interior, an indoor lap pool flanked by exotic plantings, and an aerie amid the treetops from which he could gaze up at the sky. He also asked that the roofs be treated as a fifth elevation that would look appealing as he flew in, and he requested a clearing in the forest that would allow a helicopter to hover before landing.

The architect paced the site and returned to his Albuquerque, New Mexico, base, telling his client: "If I put pencil to paper right away, it blocks all my creativity. So I sit around for three months and think about it, and all of a sudden the design comes to me." Three months later Prince told Skilken the plans were ready. "I looked at them, and even though it's my business, I couldn't deci-

pher them," Skilken admits. "Then he showed me renderings and, finally, a huge model. As I began to understand what it would look like, I realized I didn't like it at all." He sent a letter to Prince, who agreed to produce a new design.

Three months elapsed before Prince gave Skilken a roll of plans, and this time the response was enthusiastic. "Bart listens to you, changes things quite readily, and doesn't let his ego get in the way," says the client. Local inspectors had never seen anything like the plans, but they issued approvals based on an independent engineer's assessment that the structure would stand firm.

To prepare the site, Prince dammed a creek in a ravine, turning it into an ornamental pond, and located the house at the top of the slope, with a helipad at its base. To the east, another depression was excavated to provide limestone for building, and this, too, was flooded to serve as a recreational lake. On the plan, the house appears as a cluster of circles, the largest of which has been cut in half, flanked by a circular entrance court and a curved ramp leading down to the drive-through garage and a shelter for the helicopter, which is drawn inside on rails

ABOVE: A red canvas canopy shades the auto court, which is reached by a circular drive. "Stone walls cut into the ground, above which hovers the light-framed structure of the sheltering copper and glass roofs," says Prince.

OPPOSITE: A seventy-five-foot-long pool winds its way along the lower level of the house. "The owner wanted a lap pool running through a tropical garden, with palm trees and bananas and views of the sky," the architect says. "The living spaces are arranged around that."

LEFT: Beams radiate from a central column in the main living area. Above it is the storm room; below, accessible by a ramp, are the pool and garden areas. Inside the column are the house's mechanical and electrical systems. Sandstone quarried on-site was used for the fireplace, at rear.

from its round landing pad. All of these curves, and those of the laminated beams that support the vaults, are precisely calculated to achieve a harmonious symmetry. The hundreds of panes of glass, covering three-quarters of the exterior surface, presented a greater challenge. Each required a separate template and had to be precisely fitted to withstand the extremes of the Ohio climate. In contrast, the masons had to be urged repeatedly to make the walls rough and irregular. Despairing of their willingness to abandon their customary exactitude, Skilken suggested they drink beer before laying the stones.

From the granite-paved forecourt one enters the house at its middle level. Brazilian cherry bridges and stairways lead through open cages of laminated-pine beams, linking semi-enclosed areas within the light-filled space. There is a view down through plate-glass balustrades to a seventy-five-foot-long serpentine pool lined with mirror-and-glass mosaic, which was laid by a pair of craftsmen from Mexico. The pool is surrounded by sandstone layers, lime and banana trees, and lofty palms. Three wedge-shaped guest suites radiate from a spiral stairway ascending to the master suite. To the left of the

ABOVE: Prince sculpted the site "to form hidden lower levels" and shored it up with stone walls. Bananas, papayas, guavas, and other tropical fruits and flowers grow in the garden, which is enclosed in a domed conservatory near the man-made pond and waterfall.

LEFT: The master bedroom, which has a private balcony, is set at the top of a spiral staircase that links the four rooms in the bedroom wing.

entrance is a walkway to an open-sided living/dining area, with steps leading up to a round kitchen. Suspended above both is a belvedere/bar that Skilken calls his storm room—a place to enjoy rainy weather or a full moon through the glass ceiling vault. The upstairs rooms open onto roof terraces, which gave Skilken a romantic setting for proposing to his wife, Karen.

Though they subsequently had a child and had to baby-proof these vertiginous spaces, Skilken continues to describe the house as a place for big kids. Secret passageways are hidden within the masonry walls, and the kitchen's refrigerator and microwave are mounted on an elevator that carries them down to the pool or up to the storm room.

To keep the plants healthy, the glass is unscreened and natural light floods in, bringing the labyrinthine interior into relief and adding a warm glow to wood and stone. When night falls, a constellation of tiny lights sparkles off the glass and heightens the sense of mystery. And yet, for all its complexities, the house is surprisingly compact, and its living areas seem intimate, thanks to the arced beams that embrace them. It also reaches out to the landscape, pulling in vistas of nature to complement the sophisticated artifice within.

"We wanted everything to be transparent, not translucent," Prince says. "There are almost no blinds, draperies, or *brise-soleils*." RIGHT: Windowpanes, which cover three-quarters of the exterior, enclose the storm room. Glass guardrails "join the spaces visually."

Between a Rock and a Hard Place in Utah

Carving a Playful Hideaway from the Rugged Canyonlands Outside Moab

Architecture and Interior Design by Dick Knecht
Text by Steven M. L. Aronson
Photography by Mary E. Nichols

A western cabin—that's how entrepreneur John Hauer and his wife, Nancy, a former college administrator, envisioned the vacation house they were about to build in the canyonlands of Utah. But their designer, Aspen-based Dick Knecht, demurred—he fancied the house wearing the picturesque and sentimental face of a frontier whorehouse. "The kind of place where you hitched your horses up," he rhapsodized, "and there was a front porch, and a bar and gambling on the ground floor, and the whores lived upstairs in little rooms with balconies, and you could always count on having a good fistfight and the bad guys would fall down the stairs and break the railings." As the structure went up, Knecht would say, triumphantly, "We're building a whorehouse!" and Hauer would laugh, "You mean a Hauer house." So, homophonically, the house came to be known as—indeed, John and Nancy would have T-shirts printed up proclaiming it—"The Best Little Hauer House in Utah."

The Hauers live most of the year on their fifteen-hundred-acre Turkey Track Ranch in the Black Hills of South Dakota, in a meandering house also designed for them by Knecht. (As it happens, he went to grade school in Rapid City with Nancy. "He was three years ahead of

RIGHT: A house designed by Dick Knecht for John and Nancy Hauer features a bridge leading from the master bedroom to an adjacent rock. "It's a favorite area for coffee or campfires," Knecht says. Fisher Towers rise beyond, at left. The horses are the Hauers' Peruvian Pasos.

OPPOSITE: An antler-framed mirror is mounted on the wall above a horn legged table in the entrance area. They bought the storm-pattern Navajo rug from a local trader. "You collect rugs like you collect horses—they just sort of come to you," says Nancy.

BELOW: In the living room, the bright buffalo-plaid-upholstered furnishings and a contemporary bronze contrast with the ancient rock and the rustic pine-log framing.

BELOW RIGHT: Where additional stone was needed, as in the upstairs study, it was mortared in the manner of the Anasazi cliff dwellings. "The native pine and local logs are from the La Sal Mountains, which can be seen in the distance," says Knecht.

me—he beat me up a lot," she chuckles.) The couple travel from their house in South Dakota to their house in Utah the old-fashioned way—they drive. "It's fifteen hours, with the horses," says Hauer. "They're Peruvian Pasos, known for their natural gait, which makes them just about the smoothest riding horses."

John and Nancy had been scouting the country looking for a desert location to build their house—they had covered Arizona, New Mexico, and West Texas before exploring Utah. "We saw Moab on the map and thought we'd stop there to rest the horses we were pulling, but after one look we never left," Hauer recounts. When he called Knecht in Aspen to say that he had at last found the topography of his heart's desire and, what's more, purchased roughly a hundred acres of it, Knecht was both astonished and not surprised—he knew the Moab area well and had just returned from a biking and back-packing trip there, awed anew by its sober, lonely beauty. "I dropped everything and went back to help them find a site," he recalls. "We set out on horseback, and when we found the perfect spot we got off our horses, which were standing in what is now the living room."

Knecht and the Hauers all knew the second they beheld the brace of monster rocks spaced forty feet apart—the bigger one half the size of a football field—that the house should be built between them. They saw,

too, that the natural opening in the smaller rock should be the living room window.

From their chosen site the view opens out and up—to the thousand-foot-high spires of Fisher Towers and Castle Rock; to the Colorado River flowing in its breadth beside the property; to Adobe Mesa, Porcupine Rim, Power Pole Rim, the snow-crowned La Sal Mountains, and, across the river, a corner of Arches National Park. "It's real Marlboro country," Hauer sums up. The terrain, though desert, is green not only in summer—thanks to flowering cacti and to the willows, cottonwoods, and tamarisk on the river—but in winter, thanks to the rampant juniper trees, which never shed.

Knecht got right to work making conceptual drawings for a project that he describes today as "the smallest I've ever done, but the most fun." Hauer adds, "It turned into not the western cabin we'd had in mind but just what we had wanted all along without knowing it until Dick showed us." It was the Hauers' contractor, Jim Foy, who took Knecht's concept and put it into wood and plaster and stone; he literally sculpted the house, molded it into the rock. "To Jim, nothing was impossible," Hauer marvels. "He said, 'There has to be a way to make that window fit between those rocks.' Most builders would have framed it with wood. And it would have looked tacky."

Foy's solution was to make a plywood pattern for the gigantic piece of glass—twenty feet tall, eighteen feet wide, and made up of three sections—and ship it to a glassmaker in California with an oven big enough to temper it (only after being cut could it be tempered). Back in Moab, Foy embedded the glass two inches into the Hauers' rock and sealed it around the edges with concrete made from sand from the rock itself so the color would match exactly. "I can't tell you how much the window there looks like you don't have a window there," Hauer says. "People walk in the front door and stare out—they don't see glass, they think we just have this opening in the rock. And I say, 'Yeah, when we save enough money we're going to put some glass in.'"

The façade of the house was built six feet above the roofline and squared off to look like an authentic Wild West building. "That's the way the old westerners built most of the bars and hardware stores and blacksmith shops and whorehouses—with false fronts on them," Hauer points out. The indefatigable Foy went on to embellish the top of the façade with period architectural moldings and details (he had to fashion the tools himself in order to make these embellishments).

The downstairs consists simply of a big two-story balconied living room with ceilings twenty-four feet high and a small kitchen at the far end. Foy made all the cabinets out of the same native pine he'd used for the inside of the house. "Our house can truly be said to be a product of its surroundings—the wood came from the nearby La Sal Mountains," Hauer observes, proudly adding, "The same as the early settlers did, we used the natural things." A straight-run pine staircase leads to a large bedroom and a study; a smaller bedroom was carved out of a section of balcony. "We're going to hang a rope from the log beam in the ceiling of the little bedroom down through the trapdoor next to the rock that makes up the wall, so our grandson, who's now two, can take his first rock-climbing lesson, going all the way," Hauer laughs, "from the bedroom to the living room." He and Nancy each have a bath: Hers flaunts one of the whorehouse windows in the front; his has been opened wide to the view of Fisher Towers.

Fittingly, the fabric on the chairs, footstools, and bedcoverings in this western house is buffalo plaid. As for carpeting, Nancy recalls: "Dick said, 'In this house we'll have no carpeting.' And I said, 'Of course we're going to have carpeting.'" In the end, these two friendly antagonists from grade school compromised: The big bedroom has bright, almost fire-engine red carpeting (the whorehouse effect), which, however, can't be seen from the living room. The Hauers regard as "one of the furnishings of the house" a Carlos Nakai tape of Navajo flute music; they keep it running twenty-four hours a day up on the balcony. "People will be in our house for an hour and then suddenly start listening to it, it's so subtle," Hauer says. "It floats around the house and sounds like it's coming from everywhere."

The main house was not even completed when the Hauers decided to add another building to their small frontier town: a one-story, twenty-by-twenty-five-foot guesthouse, to be called The Outpost and located just a hundred yards away. (Later two barns, sporting the same old-western-style false fronts as the house, and four corrals—two on the river—would be built out of pine poles and cedar posts.) Digging six feet for the guesthouse foundation, Foy found arrowheads, pottery shards, layers of charcoal from ancient fires, and metates, the stones that the Anasazi had ground their grain on. "The local archaeologist told us she's pretty sure this site has been continuously occupied for four thousand years," says Hauer. The Outpost is furnished with period western furniture, including a headboard with eight Mexican spurs embedded in it, their rowels sticking up. To Hauer, "it looks like John Wayne just left."

And in a way, he has. Moab can boast of having once been the uranium capital of the world, but it was a

BELOW: "Old West towns and the site's movie history were my inspiration," says Knecht. "I thought modeling the house after a classic whorehouse would be perfect."

much-mined movie location, too. Hauer went to the ardent trouble of sorting out just which parts of just which films were shot on his property; then he stitched together a video of them for himself. "In *Rio Grande*, there's a shot of John Wayne and Maureen O'Hara standing a few feet from what's now our big window," he says. "John Ford, who directed that movie, fell in love with this place—he also shot *Wagonmaster* here. And in *The Comancheros*, John Wayne shoots a bad guy off the rock that now forms the main wall of our house." Nor is movie-making in Moab a thing of the past. "Some of *Thelma & Louise* was filmed here," Hauer points out. "Right near the end, when they skid to a stop at the edge of the cliff and their terror turns to wonder—well, what they see through their windshield is what we see out our living room."

Hauer often stays up till 2:00 A.M. reading history and geology books about the area. In the day he sometimes bakes bread, and he and Nancy ride, clean corrals, and do a lot of hiking. Nancy says, "Our redbone hound—his name is Blender because he's red and the rocks are red—sings to us early in the morning. We hike and he sings."

Hauer stresses, "Our 'Little Hauer House' isn't an escape *from* anything—the Black Hills of South Dakota are beautiful, too. It's an escape *to* something. To a different world: the world of geology, the world of the Anasazi, the desert. At night we sit in front of the big window and turn the lights out, and for the first minutes you see only a black hole, then some stars, then hundreds and thousands of stars, then the outline of Fisher Towers."

Call it the poetry of space.

ABOVE: "I wanted to create a hideaway deep in the canyonlands," says Knecht. The surrounding countryside has been used in films ranging from *Rio Grande* to *Thelma & Louise*. A prominent feature of the house is the window created from a natural opening in the rock.

New York Primaries

Bold Forms for an Architect's Own Bridgehampton Residence

Architecture by Preston T. Phillips
Text by Pilar Viladas
Photography by Paul Warchol

Among the shingle-and-clapboard cottages that crowd the woods and onetime potato fields of Long Island's Bridgehampton, architect Preston T. Phillips's house is a surprise. What emerges at the end of his winding, tree-lined driveway is no tasteful exercise in contextuality. Instead, a bright red cube knitted to a yellow box by a red-and-yellow checkerboard seam stands a short distance from a brilliant blue pyramid. At first glance it looks like a child's exuberant drawing of a house; in reality it is a sophisticated, considered design by an architect who knows his craft.

When flying over the Hamptons one day, Phillips was captivated by the sight of the sun glinting off a pond in a heavily wooded area. It took him a year to find that pond again—the place was so overgrown—but his perseverance paid off. Phillips knew that the gently rolling oasis would be the perfect site for the vibrant, sculptural buildings he had in mind for his residence and studio. "I couldn't see this house plunked down in the middle of a field," he says. "I wanted it to appear from out of nowhere, like Falling-water or Monticello."

From the front, the stucco-covered main structure is almost monolithic. Its solid surface is broken only by the fiberglass panels, tinted red and yellow, that act as a "zipper," as the architect puts it, uniting the two sections of the house. The red cube contains the living room, dining area, and kitchen on the first floor and the master bedroom on the second. The yellow box accommodates a guest bedroom on the first floor and a study above, the latter connected to the master bedroom by a bridge that spans

OPPOSITE: The pyramid-shaped studio in architect Preston T. Phillips's Bridge-hampton, New York, residential compound is a striking presence in a woodland setting bordered by irises.

LEFT: The fiberglass panels that join the two sections of the house "add a certain kinetic quality," Phillips notes. Marked by the colored squares on two sides and overhead, the double-height entrance atrium is on axis with the dining terrace.

"I chose the colors and forms for their purity and timelessness," says Phillip. "The pieces had to respond to the site's primal character." RIGHT: On a bluestone dining terrace, Canadian Adirondack-style chairs, circa 1933, surround an Italian-designed table.

the skylit entrance atrium. The southside elevation is dominated by a trapezoidal glass enclosure attached to the red cube. This steel framed, canted roof defines the "sky room," a soaring space, as much greenhouse as living room, that is set a few steps below grade to face directly into the garden.

The interior volumes are meant to appear "totally carved out," according to Phillips. While some walls are painted the same shades as the exterior—the palette of primary colors was inspired by early-twentieth-century art movements such as de Stijl and Russian Suprematism—most are gray or black, the better to visually recede and provide a foil for the architect's collection of contemporary art. "The black walls have the effect of negative space," he explains. "They come off as unlit voids rather than walls."

In keeping with the spirit of the open plan, there are only two doors inside the house—one for the guest bedroom, the other for the powder room. The master bedroom floats above the first floor, gaining light from the

living room and the double-height atrium. A panel of black mesh screening in the bedroom conceals track lighting, creating a ceiling—visible from the living spaces below—that is opaque by day and translucent at night.

The bold volumes, particularly the living room, reveal the influence of Phillips's mentor, the formidable modernist architect Paul Rudolph. Phillips joined Rudolph's office in New York following architecture school at Auburn University. ("I went to see the chapel he designed in Tuskegee," he recalls, "and it knocked my socks off. I knew that this was who I was going to work for.") Of his three years with Rudolph, Phillips says, "It was like graduate school every day. He was always teaching." After going off on his own, Phillips spent several more years in New York, doing lofts and commercial projects, before heading out to Long Island to seek "a quieter life."

Not only does he have that, but the commute to work isn't bad either—across the front lawn to an airy, art-filled studio in the blue pyramid. The striking pair of

"As dictated by Kandinsky, I used yellow but used it sparingly," Phillips says. LEFT: The composition of planes edging the dining area includes the sliding red door to the guest bedroom. The portrait of Roy Lichtenstein is by John MacWhinnie; the acrylic is by Tom Slaughter.

geometric solids occupies a landscape as carefully planned by Phillips as the architecture: "The garden was one of the first conceptual sketches I did," he says. It was designed to offer beautifully framed views of nature from every room. Dogwoods form an axial backdrop for the dining terrace at the rear; a weeping cherry tree "looks like a fountain of water," Phillips observes, against the taut lines of the living room window. The living room also surveys the small pond, which is now home to a nude sculpture by Lowell Nesbitt and is bordered by Japanese yellow flag irises.

The yellow of the house further carries over to the garden with a broad band of daylilies—and in the spring, what Phillips describes as "fireworks displays" of forsythia. For the architect, the question was, "Where do you want the eye to go?" The property was so dense, "there needed to be a green platform for the house to sit on," he says. "After that, the gardens could be serpentine."

The complex is particularly dramatic at night, when it glows from within. Light punches through the checkerboard and the faceted glazing of both structures, making a lantern-dotted glen. Phillips delights in the fact that, washed by uplights, the house's façade reminds him of the curtain at the Art Deco movie theater in the town where he grew up—proof that even the most committed of modernists is not immune to the charms of the past.

ABOVE: The geometric solids—the red-and-yellow house and the blue pyramidal studio—are, Phillips says, "elemental shapes that are both grounding and liberating in how I live and work."

LEFT: "At night," Phillips says of the uplit front facade, "the scale is such that you can't tell its size, and that makes it wonderfully mysterious."

OPPOSITE: The living room "thrusts itself into the landscape," says Phillips, who set the Corian surround behind the built-in sofas level with the garden. Black anodized-steel framing reinforces and defines the sloped roof and wall.

Ralph Lauren's Bedford Beauty

The Designer Envisions a True Gentleman's Retreat in New York

Text by Stephen Drucker
Photography by Durston Saylor

The "RL" on the pillowcases is not a logo. These rooms do not have the Ralph Lauren "look."

Ralph Lauren and his family live here, in Bedford, New York, in a house we have all wondered about for years but have never before seen so completely. It is one of five Lauren houses, and an especially interesting one, the one closest to his oldest and most powerful image, the American gentleman.

To fully appreciate it you must try not to think about the store windows and displays you know so well. This is not a stage; it is not about selling; this is where Ricky and Ralph Lauren have lived for thirteen years and where they have raised three children. It is their home, and in the realm of interior design it is very much an original. There is no need to search for social meaning in it, as often happens when the subject turns to Lauren. Quite simply, it is English in flavor but with an American energy, and whether Nancy Mitford would approve or not is irrelevant. By now we should all understand that this is an interpretation of Englishness, not a re-creation of it.

What is important here is that only this designer, with his particular style radar, the man who gave us the oxford-cloth button-down pillowcase and the wingtip brogue wing chair, could take the symbols of a civilized life and arrange them into so potent an interior. The atmosphere in this house is intense, like breathing pure

"It's a combination hunting lodge and stately home," Ralph Lauren says of the residence he and his wife, Ricky, share in Bedford, New York. LEFT: The Norman-style stone manor house dates to 1919. A pair of vintage automobiles from his collection occupies the circular drive.

oxygen. It goes to your head. If Lauren brings any interior designer to mind, it is Renzo Mongiardino, whose rooms also were never quite the sum of fabric and wood. It is hard to look at rooms like these without wanting to know what music is playing, which books are being read, how the flowers are arranged, which shoes are in the dressing room. Let's take a walk through them together and find out.

Ricky and Ralph Lauren live about an hour north of Manhattan in a village that is to suburbs as the navy cashmere blazer is to men's jackets. To call Bedford a suburb is somewhat misleading; it is more like Manhasset or Old Westbury in the day of the Paleys and the Phipps. Zoning is generous, houses are hidden, and horses are welcome.

The paved road gives way to dirt and gravel several miles short of the Lauren residence, which is surrounded by over 250 acres of rolling lawn and woods. Norman in style, stone, and slate, it was built in 1919, and there is no reason to think it will look any different a hundred years from now. At seventeen thousand square feet it is big but not overwhelming; it feels appropriate and comfortable. The only clue to who is in residence is the car in the forecourt, one of a collection of classic sports cars that look as they did the day they were delivered a half century ago.

As in an English "stately," the entrance hall is not overly decorated. A grandly scaled George II side table and the first of many oil paintings greet you, as does the scent of lilies. Throughout the house there are dense, formal arrangements of romantic white flowers—

ABOVE: Prominent paintings in the dining room include, from right, *A Woman Hunting*, nineteenth century, by Alfred Dedreux; Henry Koehler's 1927 *Hunting Coats and Whips of the Pytchley Hunt Staff*; and *Piebald Horse in a Field*, nineteenth century, by Thomas Moyford. Ralph Lauren Home flatware.

RIGHT: Dominating a corner of the master sitting room is a Louis XV *bureau plat*, attributed to Jacques Dubois, from the collection of Edmond de Rothschild. Tartan accessories, found in nearly all the major rooms, top the desk. The plaid fabric is from Ralph Lauren Home.

RIGHT: A circa 1860 English chandelier illuminates the living room. Above the George II table is an eighteenth-century tapestry. The zebra wing chairs are Louis XV. Hanging between the windows is a portrait of James Ransey Cuthbert, painted by Sir Thomas Lawrence around 1805–10.

hydrangeas, imperial lilies, calla lilies—with old-fashioned scarlet-red roses tucked into them.

The hall opens on the left to a library, a mahogany-paneled room that leaves an impression of brawny club furniture and perpetual late afternoon. The usual laptop and BlackBerry are nowhere in sight, though pads and sharp pencils are plentiful. To the right is the dining room, with a George III table receding forever across three pedestals, vermeil flatware, and a dense hang of paintings and drawings against deep-green velvet walls. One end of the first floor is occupied by a classic English drawing room. The center table stands under a crystal chandelier by Osler; seating groups hug fireplaces at either end; and despite paintings propped against paintings, car-

pets layered upon carpets, and towers of books, the mood is light.

Certain themes keep appearing. Lauren likes his rooms deeply colored, highly dramatic, and turned inward. He prefers mahogany paneling and Georgian furniture polished like glass, and Persian carpets on their way to threadbare. Tartan, which most interior designers regard as a novelty, seems natural to a fashion person and is used with abandon. The dining room draperies are like great fringed kilts; tartan pillows and throws and runners are everywhere; and there are many collections of antique plaid metal boxes and accessories.

Animal imagery, and the energy it imparts, is everywhere too, in pencil studies of lions and oil paintings of

ABOVE: The master bedroom, which is enveloped in a deep-blue fabric, is anchored by a Georgian mahogany-and-walnut bureau-cabinet and an eighteenth-century mahogany armchair by Georges Jacob. A Regency bed, chinoiserie accents, and Oriental rugs round out the mix of styles.

LEFT: A circular mahogany-paneled hall leads to the master bath, part of the Laurens' five-room upstairs master suite. The couple chose white marble for the space, which overlooks the grounds, and incorporated a mirrored wall and an eighteenth-century mantelpiece.

RIGHT: Lauren's closet and dressing room are outfitted with mahogany millwork. Classic pieces such as riding boots and jean jackets are part of his everyday wardrobe.

horses and leopards, and especially in the designer's fascination with leather. Lauren collects leather the way an anthropologist collects bones. It is almost always what you find yourself sitting on. Old briefcases and school-bags are used as accessories. Hide, suede, alligator, and croc turn up in every possible condition: nicely mellowed, worn to a shine, darkened from a century of fingertips, shaped to the human form, crumbling to dust. This is a museum of leather.

The Laurens' private quarters, a five-room suite opening off a paneled round hall, are upstairs. The bedroom, with walls of deep-blue baize that read like the midnight sky at full moon, has furniture somewhat dressier than the rest of the house. The bed is Regency, and on the table next to it there's a pocket watch, tortoiseshell accessories, and crystal tumblers with a bottle of San Pellegrino. Next door is a sitting room, used primarily by

Ricky Lauren, mixing tartans liberally with a very French desk glowing with ormolu. The bath, with the marble tub at the center facing an eighteenth-century mantelpiece, gives the illusion of an old bedroom converted when indoor plumbing was introduced a century ago.

In every house you must search a little to find the heartbeat. Often it is in the kitchen or library. In the Lauren house the life force beats strongest in the dressing room, with its green baize walls, highly polished mahogany, and the luxurious hush of so much beautiful clothing. Stacks of luggage surround the room, like magnificent old saddles in a stable. There is a shelf of leather boots as interesting as any collection of Chinese vases, a wall of cashmere sweaters mostly in navies and grays, and another wall of nicely broken-in Belgian loafers, all monogrammed "RL." Here Ralph Lauren says good morning to Ralph Lauren.

The Laurens, below left, shuttle between the Bedford retreat and a summer house in Montauk, New York; a Manhattan town house, a villa in Jamaica; and the sixteen-thousand-acre Double RL Ranch in Colorado.

OPPOSITE: The poolhouse terrace.

ABOVE: The spacious lawn and ivy-covered walls of the seventeen-thousand-square-foot house, surrounded by greenery and sitting on more than two hundred and fifty acres, evoke an estate in the English countryside.

Gilded Age Glory

Mr. and Mrs. William K. Vanderbilt's Marble House in Newport

Architecture by Richard Morris Hunt
Text by John A. Cherol
Photography by Derry Moore

"It is as much as a man's brain can do to keep up with the Vanderbilt work." Thus Richard Morris Hunt, considered the dean of nineteenth-century American architecture, wrote toward the end of his life about the family that had kept him most busy during his extraordinarily active career. Within that large and diverse clan, whose patronage was unmatched in its time, one figure stood out in the architect's mind: Mrs. William Kissam Vanderbilt.

"Richard had the greatest admiration for Mrs. William K. Vanderbilt's intellect and broad grasp of architecture," Hunt's wife, Catharine, wrote shortly after his death. "And he often said: 'She is a wonder!'"

This collaboration between the academically trained Hunt and the rising queen of American society, Alva Smith Vanderbilt, was remarkable from the first. Hunt's introduction to the Vanderbilts came in 1878 when she commissioned him to build Idlehour—a huge Long Island retreat. A year later, he was put to work building a copy of the Château de Blois, which, when completed in 1882,

occupied a full block on New York's Fifth Avenue. As one of the first examples of Beaux-Arts residential architecture to appear in the United States, it caused a sensation, drew rave reviews, and propelled the Vanderbilts unimpeachably into the exclusive ranks of New York's Four Hundred.

The most dazzling of their commissions, however, was the Marble House in Newport, Rhode Island. Hunt's original drawings for this residence (now in the collection of the American Institute of Architects in Washington, D.C.) reveal an extraordinary dialogue between architect and patron. According to Catharine, Mrs. Vanderbilt spent many hours with the architect and his draftsmen, poring over drawings, researching details, correcting specifications, and precisely noting her comments on the presentation drawings as well as on the finished plans. No detail eluded her scrutiny.

Mrs. Vanderbilt's motivation in building Marble House was undoubtedly to improve her social position.

In 1889, the renowned Richard Morris Hunt, a founder of the American Institute of Architects, designed one of the grandest of Newport, Rhode Island's "summer cottages"—Marble House—for Mr. and Mrs. William K. Vanderbilt. OPPOSITE: Allegorical bronze figures, flanking a clock in the form of terrestrial and celestial globes, surmount the *fleur-de-pêche* mantel in the Gold Salon.

RIGHT: Inspiration for the white marble façade came from the eighteenth-century Petit Trianon at Versailles and the White House.

LEFT: With golden-hued hangings and wallcovering, and a late-eighteenth-century Aubusson carpet, one of the most sumptuous rooms in Marble House is Mrs. Vanderbilt's bedroom—a regal setting in a Baroque spirit.

When the first drawings appeared on Hunt's drafting tables, the Vanderbilts were one of the two wealthiest couples in the United States, a distinction they shared with William's older brother, Cornelius Vanderbilt, and his wife.

Given Mrs. Vanderbilt's virtually unlimited budget and consuming interest in architecture, design, and the decorative arts, Marble House became a logical extension of her studies, an encapsulated history of French design. Each room was her personal essay on a particular style or a specific historic interior.

The Gothic Room, in the style she thought was associated with Francis I, housed a famous collection of sixteenth-century Italian paintings, reliquaries, prints, and rare medieval stained glass. The dining room was a scaled-down copy of the Salon of Hercules at Versailles, with rose Numidian marble walls, massive gilt-bronze trophy plaques, and a court portrait of Louis XIV acquired through the famous dealer Joseph Duveen. It was stunning even by Newport standards, and was surpassed only by the adjacent Gold Salon—Mrs. Vanderbilt's version of the Hall of Mirrors at Versailles. Here, the hand-carved oak paneling, covered with thousands of sheets of gold leaf, provided the backdrop for many of Mrs. Vanderbilt's most spectacular galas. The room is a

remarkable monument to the spirit and audacity of America's Gilded Age.

Allard of Paris was the major design firm that contributed to the decorative detailing, and its metalsmiths, stone carvers, wood carvers, and other craftsmen worked prodigiously to complete the residence in a mere two years. It was then the custom to have most furnishings made to order, and those at Marble House were beautifully executed in eighteenth-century styles by the firms of Sourmani and André Dasson of Paris.

The studied opulence and regal splendor of Mrs. Vanderbilt's summer cottage impressed her friends but often overwhelmed her family. Her daughter, Consuelo, wrote about her mother's architectural achievement, undertaken with Hunt and inspired by the Petit Trianon at Versailles: "Unlike Louis XV's creation, it stood in restricted grounds and, like a prison, was surrounded by high walls." She went on to give a glimpse of the style her mother enforced within: "Writing utensils were disposed in such perfect order that I never ventured to use them, for my mother had chosen every piece of furniture and placed every ornament according to her taste . . . "

Marble House's lavish style set a frantic pace for Newport cottage architecture from 1892 onward and played a substantial role in Mrs. Vanderbilt's plan to marry

ABOVE: Named for its lavish marble interiors, the house features a luxurious dining room of rose Numidian marble. A portrait of Louis XIV by Pierre Mignard I graces the overmantel. The room, enhanced with gilded ornamentation and furnished with gilt-bronze chairs upholstered in velvet woven with gold thread, is based on the Salon of Hercules at Versailles.

OPPOSITE: Intricate tracery embellishes the chimney-piece, ceiling, and windows of the Gothic Room—designed by Hunt after Mrs. Vanderbilt's interpretation of the style of Francis I. Originally, the room housed a collection of reliquaries and sixteenth-century paintings, and the windows were set with stained glass.

her daughter to a major European aristocrat. Having been royally wined and dined as a houseguest, the duke of Marlborough married Consuelo Vanderbilt shortly after, in 1895.

Though Mrs. Vanderbilt divorced Vanderbilt in 1896 and ceased to live at Marble House until after the death of her second husband, Oliver Hazard Perry Belmont, in 1908, she considered Marble House a major extension of her personality. When she returned to the house in the summer of 1909, she was still a leader of society but had also become the first president and one of the founders of the National Organization of Women. Marble House figured prominently as an organizational hub for this new cause. On August 22, 1909, she shocked old Newport and provided tremendous local interest by opening Marble House to the public, with fees going to the cause of women's suffrage. From then on, Marble House was the scene of lectures, workshops, and teas for the movement.

In 1912, seventeen years after the death of Hunt, Mrs. Vanderbilt Belmont hired his sons, Joseph and Richard Howland Hunt, to add the Chinese Teahouse. It was finished in July 1914—in time for a rally of two thousand suffragettes and, a few days later, a party for Newporters.

At the end of that summer season, she closed Marble House and moved to the south of France, never to return to Newport. The house remained shuttered until she sold it, shortly before her death in 1932, to Mr. and Mrs. Frederick H. Prince. The Princes resided there until 1964, when the house was purchased for the Preservation Society of Newport County with funds donated by Harold S. Vanderbilt, the youngest son of Mr. and Mrs. William K. Vanderbilt. All of the original custom-designed Marble House furnishings were a gift of the Frederick H. Prince Trust.

The house stands today as a remarkable reminder of the capabilities of Hunt and the extraordinary lady who was, as contemporary wit Harry Lehr said, "only happy when . . . knee-deep in mortar."

RIGHT: Used for teas and receptions, the Chinese Teahouse, designed by Richard Howland Hunt and Joseph Howland Hunt, was completed in 1914. It was adapted from a small temple in Hunan Province, China.

Glass Geometries

An Architect's Bold Vision Overlooking the Sea of Japan

Architecture by Shoei Yoh
Text by Carol Lutfy
Photography by Jaime Ardiles-Arce

Architect Shoei Yoh designed a glass-and-concrete retreat for his family on an ocean bluff near Fukuoka, Japan. OPPOSITE: Marble steps lead to the south entrance, where a Charles Rennie Mackintosh chair anchors the glass-enclosed, suspended space.

By anyone's standards, it was a spectacular plot of land. But for an architect interested in exploring the relationship between buildings and nature, it was the opportunity of a lifetime.

Japanese architect Shoei Yoh and his wife, Kimiko, found the property in the town of Shimomachi after an unflagging ten-year search. Located on a bluff about 450 feet above sea level, it commanded a breathtaking view of the Sea of Japan, of the distant Tsushima and Ikinoshima islands, and of a lush green hilly coastline. Best of all, there was not a hint in sight that Fukuoka, the largest city on the island of Kyushu, was only twenty miles away.

The Yohs purchased the land (formerly a cattle ranch) in 1983 in the hope of transforming it into a weekend getaway. Unsure at first of how to proceed, they sat on the property—literally—for eight years. Spreading out a straw mat or two, the couple and their two children held a picnic on the site at least once every month. There they pondered how to respect the surrounding splendor while reaping the rewards of the view.

Yoh's fundamental impulse was to create a primitive dwelling. He considered, for instance, replacing the picnic mats with an open-air platform or constructing a simple shelter like a watchtower. These ideas, although impractical for a family of four, ultimately formed the basis for his final plan: to build the closest thing possible to an invisible structure—what he calls "a glass house between sea and sky."

For the fifty-five-year-old award-winning architect, the prospect of erecting a glass house reverberated with both historical and personal significance. For one thing, it was the second glass house he had designed for his family.

RIGHT: Two concrete walls secure the structure to the site.

LEFT: "Like anyone else, we wanted furniture and art and music," Yoh says, "but we had to respect the simplicity and neutrality of the overall design." Yoh's furniture designs for the living/dining room include the dining table, the cubistic sofas (which are also used for storage: "I played with the form to achieve function as well as a minimal presence"), and the pyramid-shaped glass shelves. Among his concessions to the climate are a heated floor and weatherproof paint on the raw concrete. "While the whole idea was a fusion with nature, you can't just have nature. One by one we added the things we love, and the space became vivid and warm and lively."

OPPOSITE: "Borders between sea and sky become lost in the darkness," says Yoh. Protruding eastward, the cantilevered living room "embraces all the drama that nature offers," he remarks. "At night we look out onto the old fishing boats with their lanterns and feel that we're one of them."

RIGHT: "My wife and I could live very comfortably in just this one room," comments Yoh of the master bedroom at the northwest corner. "It has the best views in the house, and in summer it's a great place to have dinner." A table designed by the architect sits between a Le Corbusier chair, at left, and a Marcel Breuer chair.

(The first, in Fukuoka, serves as their main residence.) And like his first, it was intended initially as a nod to Mies van der Rohe's seminal 1950 glass box, the Farnsworth House.

Somewhere along the way, though, Yoh realized that his design for the house was actually more indebted to traditional Japanese architecture. "Though I employed modernist materials, the house possesses a very Japanese feel for me," he says. "I started out with the precepts of modernism and ended up finding my Japanese roots in them.

"There was never a moment when I thought, 'I want to make something Japanese.' But in the process of building the house, I realized how much I had been influenced by everyday aspects of Japanese architecture. The ability to open and close a structure completely, the versatility of tatami—these things eased their way into my thinking."

Completed in 1991, the single-story house is a simple, elevated glass-and-concrete box that juts out over a cliff in order to take full advantage of the view. It is flanked on its south side by a small wading pool and on its north side by a marble terrace overlooking the sea. Two vertical concrete slabs, which extend boldly toward the south, anchor it in place.

Yoh's design for the house was guided largely by a desire to absorb the surrounding drama of nature: the heavy mists and pounding sunshine, the hard rains and harsh winds. "Glass itself is not usually thought of in terms of protective shelter, but it acts as an ideal picture frame for what is happening outside," he explains. "From that perspective, it is best used to integrate a structure into its environment."

In addition, Yoh found inspiration in the principles of flexibility and transparency, both integral to Japanese architecture. He says that he sees the house's central, multifunctional space in the same light as an oversize tatami room. The marble floor is heated and, like tatami, is suitable for walking barefoot. And he compares his use of glass to sliding shoji doors and to an *engawa*, or garden veranda. "Glass links the interior with the outside world," he says.

The architect, however, was not satisfied with viewing nature—he wanted the house to confront it. To a certain extent, this was an inevitable consequence of the site, which faces north and is subjected to fierce winter winds. (Given its location and elevation, it encounters the same wind pressure as a skyscraper in a typhoon area.)

But Yoh intensified the struggle between the house and the elements by experimenting with new technology and materials. The house is composed of frameless glass sheets joined together by nothing more than silicone rubber. The glass box, meanwhile, is held in place only

by suspension rods connecting it to the concrete base. Both techniques represent a first for Yoh, a circumstance that admittedly makes him concerned about safety. But, he says, "I like to experiment. For me, this is the biggest benefit of being both architect and client."

Experiments with materials have long been an integral part of Yoh's architecture—as the ride from his office in Fukuoka down the coast to his weekend house attests. Along the way, one passes his Saibu Gas Museum for Natural Phenomenart (1989), an avant-garde suspended glass-and-mirror building. A bit farther down is the Kinoshita Clinic (1979), an aluminum cylinder built to withstand wind and salt from the sea. Yoh designed the single largest timber roof in the country—an endeavor undertaken to benefit a struggling lumber town—and has just completed his first structure made from bamboo.

Yoh is self-trained, having come to architecture by way of interior design. After obtaining a degree in economics, he briefly studied fine and applied arts in the United States. He established his practice in Fukuoka in 1970 and in 1983 won both the prestigious Mainichi Design Award and the Japan Institute of Architects Award.

In addition to the structure, Yoh designed most of the furniture for the two-bedroom house, adopting a holistic approach rare among Japanese architects. "I am no longer able to differentiate between interior and architectural design," he says. "They have melded into the same thing for me."

With the exception of a few small works of art, the house has a colorless interior in which glass and shades of white and gray are deftly used to foster a sense of transparency. But this minimalism is offset—indeed, seen to advantage—by the setting. "Everything outside is magnified through the contrast with nothingness," Yoh says. "And the glass lets it all come in."

ABOVE: A glass handrail on the deck at the north end of the house maximizes the views. Though Yoh was inspired by such glass-clad Western icons of modernism as Mies van der Rohe's Farnsworth House and Philip Johnson's Glass House, he notes that glass is the material that "most serves the traditional Japanese idea of minimizing the separation between architecture and nature."

ABOVE: "The pool is a counter-weight to the house, the weight of the water essential to the suspension dynamic," says Yoh. The deck's wood slatting prevents it from buckling in the winter. To facilitate airflow, the roof is made up of fiberglass panels. "I was only after a trellis effect; the strong visual impact wasn't calculated."

RIGHT: The glass curtain wall wraps around the house from the entrance, giving a two-hundred-and-seventy-degree panorama.

Evolution in Los Angeles

A Designer Breathes New Life into a Lloyd Wright House

Interior Design by Mimi London
Text by Pilar Viladas
Photography by Mary E. Nichols

OPPOSITE: At her 1922 Lloyd Wright house in Los Angeles, Mimi London uses the central courtyard for everything from morning coffee to entertaining. Lanterns from Chinatown provide a festive note. A bignonia cascades from the balcony at right; Lloyd Wright incorporated the plant into his landscape design for his father's Hollyhock House.

For Los Angeles interior and furniture designer Mimi London, a life well lived is one that evolves. London's certainly has. After a childhood that was divided between cosmopolitan San Francisco and the wide-open spaces of northern Montana, she spent ten years as a fashion model in Paris and New York. Then, faced with deciding, as she puts it, "whether to go back to Paris and be grand or to come out to Los Angeles and have fun," London chose the latter, where she soon began designing furniture—from tree-trunk tables to log beds—that was made famous by decorating legends such as Michael Taylor. A decade ago, in an appropriate nod to the pioneering spirit that has characterized so much of twentieth-century California design, she moved into a 1922 house designed by

Lloyd Wright, son of the great American master and an accomplished architect in his own right.

True to London's credo, the house has evolved along with its owner.

The building, a rather austere composition of planes that was influenced by both Mayan and Moderne architecture, was designed by the younger Wright for Henry Bollman, and it includes some of the patterned concrete-block construction that characterized the houses Frank Lloyd Wright was creating at exactly the same time. When London bought the house, its interior block-and-plaster walls had been painted a pale yellow color, and she decided to leave them that way. But after the Northridge earthquake in 1994, the house needed some major repairs. "I

In removing layers of plaster from the walls, London found traces of gilt paint, prompting her to hand-rub the surfaces with gold. RIGHT: Whale bones and a Chilean candlestick occupy the entrance hall.

gutted a lot of it and took the plaster walls down to the lath," she explains. The removal of layers of textured plaster London calls it "whipped cream" brought the original wall planes into sharp focus. "It renewed the architecture to an extraordinary degree," she says. Inspired by this discovery, London remembered that she had once scraped away the yellow paint to find traces of gold underneath. She consulted architect Eric Lloyd Wright, Lloyd Wright's son, to find out whether his father might have used gold paint on the walls. "My father would sometimes stain the concrete blocks one color and then paint the adjacent plaster wall gold," Eric Wright recalls. "He was always experimenting in those early houses."

So London decided to carry the experiment even further by hand-rubbing the wall surfaces—even the concrete blocks—gold. Such a move might horrify die-hard preservationists, but the designer argues, "I have no interest in living in a period piece. And I don't think that Lloyd Wright would have wanted to see the structure as a dead issue. I have to bring my own self into the mix so that the house remains alive." Alive it certainly is. The glowing gilt walls were a bit of a shock even to London at first, but "within three or four days it was beige to me, only more luminous," she says. "I began to understand what Lloyd Wright was up to when he designed the house—very solid on the outside and very templelike on the inside. It was a Hollywood extravaganza, 1922 style. And the gold really shows the texture of the blocks; by night, they get very 'glamourama.'"

Furnishing the house was another aspect of the evolutionary process for London. For one thing, she says, "I'm a happier person now, and the house reflects that." The living room looks softer and more feminine; its dramatic furniture and austerely modern Japanese fabrics have been replaced by the designer's interpretations of

LEFT: "Gilding the walls was hardly something I would have done," says London. "But your own house gives you an opportunity to experiment." The chairs, of London's design, join a quartet of tables that she had cut from a standing dead spruce.

more traditional pieces, such as the living room chairs, with their "part Stickley, part Adirondack, part Frank Lloyd Wright" aesthetic and pale rose mohair upholstery. "I used to think you couldn't use pink," she says with a laugh, "but now that I'm an 'old gal,' I get to use it if I want to." For the dining room, she designed a studded suede table that was inspired by some of Lloyd Wright's furniture designs. A banquette covered in silk burlap is draped with a piece of vintage fabric with a carnation print. In the master bedroom upstairs, Chinese country cabinets—London loves their "honest joinery"—complement a London-designed bed of cast iron, with connectors made in the shape of an African bracelet she once admired.

Equal in importance to the furnishings are the objects contained within the house; they trace all the phases of the designer's life. "Ninety percent of the objects in this house mean something to me," she asserts. "They're not just accessories." Moreover, they represent London's

BELOW: Hollyhocks—"an homage to the Wrights"—and rock crystal rest on the living room mantel. The burial jars are Philippine.

attempt to "integrate my city self with my country self, my childhood with my adulthood, and a more sophisticated design approach with the fundamental qualities of things like a Native American saddle."

That's why you'll find striking rock crystal, which London used to sell in the 1960s, in the living room, along with a string of carved beads that she found on a trip to Kenya and a wood bowl from Tanzania. A beaded hide skirt, also from Tanzania, is in her dressing room. And in the spare bedroom that she uses as a "projects room" for drawing and sewing, there are pictures taken by her father, who was an accomplished amateur photographer, and paintings by Lynda Fenneman of the "line shack," a type of shelter once used by cowboys, that London owns in Montana, in addition to her family's cabin on Flathead Lake. "I've been looking at that lake since I was born," says London. "It's where I most like being and where I design most of my furniture."

London's love of animals, another important current in her life, is illustrated by the presence of a saddle she uses for cutting cattle—a favorite activity. "My current passion is horses," she declares. "I have two in L.A. and seven in Montana. Riding helps me keep whatever semblance of sanity I have left." Then there's the old tennis ball that belongs to Tobiana, her black-and-white Border collie. "She spends all day in the showroom with me," says London, "and she rides with me, too."

Weaving the various threads of her life into a seamless fabric has been a challenge that London enjoys. "One of the ways you do something original is by combining elements," she says. "And as you get older, you have more experience and you bring more to the table. I'm ten years older than I was when I moved into this house, and I'm willing to take more chances—on things like pink. There's something about getting older that allows you to feel that you can do what you want. It's a real sense of freedom."

OPPOSITE: Iron gates open to the dining room. The watercolor by Lynda Fenneman depicts London in Montana on her horse Kid. Inspired by Lloyd Wright's designs, London fashioned the studded suede table. The chandelier, another London piece, features shades of Steuben glass.

House of Cards

Niki de Saint Phalle's Tuscan Fantasy

Text by Prince Michael of Greece
Photography by Massimo Listri

In Tuscany, near the medieval village of Capalbio, stands a giant group of multicolored sculptures, in striking contrast to the rural setting. They are the work of the late Niki de Saint Phalle, descendant of an aristocratic French family with American connections on her mother's side.

De Saint Phalle's idea for the Garden of the Tarot goes back a number of years. "When I was twenty-five," she once said, "an artist friend urged me to go and see Gaudi's garden in Barcelona and promised it would change my life. I went, and sure enough it did. Ever since then I have wanted to do something of the sort.

"In a sense, my whole life has been a preparation for this project. I've visited fantasy gardens at Bomarzo, near Viterbo, and the Watts Towers in California. I did trial runs, so to speak, when I created the *Golem* in Jerusalem and the *Dragon* in Belgium. My first concept was for a mythological garden."

As it turned out, the artist's eventual choice fell on the mysterious figures of the Tarot, which had always fascinated her. "I'm convinced that the Tarot cards contain an important message for us," she said. "Their origins, for one thing, are shrouded in mystery. I think that the ancient Egyptian priests passed on their secret knowledge through the twenty-two pictorial symbols we know as the Tarot. Later, Tarot cards became very popular at all levels of society and began to be used as playing cards. As time went

Fascinated by the mystery and exoticism of the Tarot, Niki de Saint Phalle created a complex of artworks representing the ancient cards. LEFT: A detail of the Magician, Card I of the Tarot.

ABOVE: The major structures of the Tarot garden. At left, the Empress, Card III, also called the Great Goddess, in which Saint Phalle lived and worked; at center, the Magician. Background, the Falling Tower and the Emperor.

LEFT: In her design for the fireplace in her studio, Saint Phalle utilized one of her favorite materials—bits of mirror.

BELOW LEFT: In a recess in the bath, perfume bottles and a heart-shaped vase are nestled in a prismatic setting.

BELOW: A winding narrow stairway with mirrored risers leads from the studio to the bedroom. Ceramic tiles decorate the light fixture.

RIGHT: The Magician is tradi-
tionally associated with
alchemy and astrology. "He
represents primal energy in
its most creative and active
form," said Saint Phalle.

by, they shed their original meaning. Anyway, I have created my own sculptural version of the Tarot."

Saint Phalle probably drew the luckiest card in the
pack the day she mentioned her project to Marella Agnelli.
"I had known Marella before her marriage, and one day
we met by chance at St. Moritz. At one point, when we
were on a long mountain walk together, I asked Marella
if she knew of a place where I could build my fantasy garden. Later she mentioned the idea to her brothers, Prince
Carlo and Prince Nicola Caracciolo, and they said, 'Why
not do it right here?'—'right here' being the farm the
family owns in Tuscany. I had already completed a
maquette of the project, in the shape of a horseshoe, and
the site they offered me on their land had exactly the
right contour."

This generous offer chimed perfectly with Saint
Phalle's great affinity for Italy. Furthermore, an astrologer
had once told her she would create the crowning masterpiece of her life in Italy.

Once the site had been selected, the next task was to
find the financing for what was bound to be an exceed-
ingly costly project. At this point a Jacqueline Cochran
representative made a proposition for a perfume that would
carry Saint Phalle's name and be marketed worldwide.
"That deal, coming immediately after the Caracciolos'
offer, was nothing short of providential," she remarked.
The perfume was a gigantic success and provided the
money she needed.

She had begun work on the fantasy garden some time
before, in collaboration with Jean Tinguely, her former
husband and her creative associate. "Already, in 1979, he
was working on the metal framework of the first big
Tarot sculpture, copying a small maquette I had made.
You see, this fantasy garden is like a cathedral; it's the
work of many people. The Italians in general have preserved an ancestral instinct for fantasy, and people have
come from all around here to encourage me. Also, I don't
think this project could have been as beautiful anywhere

OPPOSITE: A ceramic snake looks benignly down on the bathtub, for which its encircling body forms the sides. Mirrored ceiling and shelves and white openwork walls give an illusion of ice and snow. Steps lead to the studio, which is crowded with small works in progress.

ABOVE: The curving roofline and circular windows create an intriguing silhouette in the evening.

else but Italy, because the basic materials here are incomparable. We've even constructed our own kiln, which we use to make most of the ceramics.

"I've always dreamed of living inside a sculpture, inside round shapes," she continued. "Now I have built this into my lifelong dream of a fantasy garden and have made one of the sculptures my headquarters. These days I get up at 6:30 A.M., listen to music, and go through my exercises. The workers arrive at eight. I've ended up working to the rhythm of a building site, which has totally altered my existence. Before, I lived my life in isolation; now I'm part of a collective effort." The truth of this was very evident to the visitor, who was welcomed democratically by the sound of Italian pop music blaring from a worker's transistor radio.

The constant difficulties Saint Phalle had encountered in building the garden had in no sense weakened her resolve. Far from it. She had even drawn new sources of inspiration from the experience, to such a point that she swore her hands "are radio-controlled. What I believed would be the worst disasters turned out to be spectacular successes. For instance, I wanted to put a huge hand above the card representing the Magician, who is primal energy and the masculine principle governing the universe. When the sculpture was nearly finished, I suddenly realized the hand was far too big, out of proportion to the rest of the piece. I couldn't tell Jean Tinguely that, or the

worker who helped me make it. What was I to do? Well, it occurred to me that the hand would seem less large if I covered it with pieces of mirror. That's how I discovered the special magic of mirrors, which I have used here so freely.

"Again, I wanted to depict the Emperor—who symbolizes law, fatherhood, tradition, and authority—as a castle. The right-hand corner of the castle has a tower on it, and it turned out a total catastrophe. I panicked and called up Tinguely; he took the first plane down and agreed to put one of his sculptures on top of the thing. Then he told me, 'I'm going to open up that tower,' and that's how it became the Falling Tower, which is the card of divine destruction.

"In the end I've learned an important lesson: Not only am I making the Tarot cards, I am also living them, playing with forces that must be respected. So I've developed a certain prudence in regard to the cards I choose to represent. We recently completed card XIV of the Tarot, which is Temperance, something the modern world has lost sight of. Temperance also implies integrated duality, and the guardian angel is its personification; I think that accounts for my present state of well-being."

Saint Phalle's Garden of the Tarot is a sublime folly, a match for anything built on the caprice of an eighteenth- or nineteenth-century prince. It is also a local attraction and a home as original as its creator.

"The Garden of the Tarot became part of a Franco-Italian foundation created by Marella Agnelli," she said. "Once the garden is completed, my work will be over and I'll move out. I'll go somewhere else, farther away, and start a new project.

"Among other things, this project has taught me how to go beyond what I thought were my own limitations. Ever since I started work here, I've been living outside time."

Spinning the Senses

Rethinking a Rancho Santa Fe
Residence Marked by Movement
and Light

Architectural Design and Interiors by
    Wallace E. Cunningham
Text by Joseph Giovannini
Photography by Erhard Pfeiffer

Esprit de l'escalier—wit of the staircase—afflicts architects as much as it does Frenchmen who, on the stairs leaving a party, finally think of the rejoinder they should have made inside. Architects often finish a project haunted by the idea that got away—what they would have built had they only had the budget, technology, client, time—or the on-the-spot wit. Rarely does an architect have a second chance to visit a house to redress flaws with a final say.

When Wallace E. Cunningham designed Wing House in Rancho Santa Fe, California, the first time around in 1981, he got the bones right during an inspired moment. A young, twenty-something designer with only a half year at Taliesin under his belt, he walked the hilly four-acre site with his potential client and, with the sensitivity of a water witch, spontaneously drew the idea for a plan on the ground with a branch. He was hired. The drawing, two interlocking semicircles spiraling in opposite directions from a central core, follows the geometry of two canyons that converge in a natural bowl on the site. As in a Frank Lloyd Wright design that grows out of the landscape, the house intensified rather than dominated nature.

Cunningham elaborated the basic concept in subsequent drawings, devising a house that would spin the senses of anyone inside toward the rugged hillscape through banks of windows sheltered under a fanning

RIGHT: Wing House, designed and updated by Wallace E. Cunningham, who was assisted by Peggy Walther, is defined by concentric semicircles. On a four-acre site near San Diego, the house is composed of two overlapping private wings, with the public spaces at the center.

roof. Unfortunately, Rancho Santa Fe's design review board disallowed the elegant copper roof he specified, permitting only out-of-character red tile or the rather woolly-looking shingles that were finally used. Cunningham also had to frame the plate-glass windows and skylights with wood, which made the apertures heavier than necessary for the wheeling design. Glass technology lagged behind vision.

Three sets of owners loved and lavished attention on the house, but for nearly twenty years Cunningham regretted the initial architectural compromises. By the time a midwestern couple relocating to Southern California bought Wing House and hired Cunningham to adapt it to their needs, however, building technology had finally caught up with the future, and the composition of the Rancho Santa Fe design review board had changed. Cunningham himself had matured as a designer and was better able to create disappearing details: The gesture of the house to the yard and landscape would be clearer and stronger without the visual interference of pesky eye-stopping elements. "My clients asked me to update the house and make it perfect," he says. "We didn't undertake a restoration but a reinterpretation of the core ideas in today's technology."

The architectural designer started by gutting the house. The newly arrived empty-nesters didn't need the existing suite of children's bedrooms, just a master bedroom and a guest room in the northeast wing. The couple wanted to reduce the number of rooms overall and open the floor plan for flowing space throughout the house, especially between the living/dining room and the kitchen in the central area and the library in the southwest wing. The complete revision of the plan allowed Cunningham the luxury of rethinking the house top to bottom, within the context of a basic shell that would remain unchanged. "I reduced all the elements, to return absolutely to the concept of roofs floating over radiating walls," he says.

Architecture is often a matter of inches, and Cunningham started by raising the entire roof at its high point six inches. The small difference lifted the entire space, augmenting its sense of openness. He removed the wood beams supporting the glass panes in the dramatically attenuated elliptical skylight over the fireplace, sealing the edges with invisible silicon beading. To emphasize the curving rooflines, he covered the roof with copper, as initially intended, and the shape took on the knife-edged elegance implicit in the nature of a roof tapering to a point.

OPPOSITE: "The subtle curvature of the surrounding topography is reflected in the design, which encourages constant movement from one space to another, from interior to exterior," says Cunningham. An arced masonry wall shelters the southwest wing, off the living area.

LEFT: Floating above the living and dining areas is an expansive skylight. The front door, beyond the fireplace, "avoids entry into a transitional space and allows an immediate reaction to the residence's geometry," Cunningham says.

LEFT: "The pool terrace occupies the central void created by the curve of the private wing," Cunningham explains. Access to the northeast wing is via a narrow glass-walled perimeter hall, above which a grid of clerestory windows emphasizes the residence's sweeping forms.

Cunningham removed the wall-to-wall carpets and laid creamy French limestone slabs inside and out to establish a continuous floor plane that floats seamlessly through glass walls. He designed several wool rugs in abstract patterns, woven in Nepal, and built cabinets with curved faces in the open kitchen in a rich reddish cherry that picks up the bark of manzanita bushes outside. And he widened the plate-glass panels in the window walls and took out the wood mullions. Once segmented into a faceted approximation of a curve, the glass itself is now actually bowed, and entire sections of the curving glass wall glide open on fine tracks, erasing the boundary between inside and out.

In two decades of a career built on large residences, Cunningham has also become a sculptor of water, and for Wing House he created a moon-shaped, black-bottom pool whose crescent edge aligns with the geometry of the house. The owners now delight in a private Stonehenge moment when the shadow of the curving roofline coincides exactly with the curving edge of the pool.

Once compromised by a certain coarseness, the house has emerged a thoroughbred. The frameless glass walls allow form and space to glide inside and out in smooth glissandos. Light falls overhead through skylights in bold, uninterrupted wedges that turn gyroscopically on rounded walls. This is a pavilion in the garden that explains itself through the senses, and the disappearance of the details makes the explanation eloquent. Cunningham was able to at last make the house become what it always wanted to be, since that first day, when he drew the lines in the earth. The ideal is now physical. He came back from the staircase and said just the right things.

ABOVE: In the library, the curving, concentric semi-circles create bays used to define window and door openings. "This glazing draws the eye to the exterior," comments Cunningham, "enlarging the actual interior space."

Ole Bull's Little Alhambra

The Virtuoso Musician Composes a Moorish Fantasy in Norway

Text by Elizabeth Gaynor
Photography by Kari Haavisto

Rising from the bluff of an evergreen island off Norway's west coast, an onion dome and lacy Moorish arches pierce the mist to catch the reflected brightness of the roiling clouds. In the mountain villages around the ancient trading town of Bergen, most of the structures are snug, domestic representations of practical agricultural concerns or proud bourgeois accomplishment. While an occasional house boasting a veranda of deftly carved railings or a smartly gabled roofline catches the visitor's eye, nothing nearby rivals the exotic aspect of the grand villa perched on its private island at the mouth of the fjord.

The notion of a Moorish building of Norwegian pine in this remote location is entirely in keeping with the nature of its nineteenth-century owner, famed violinist Ole Bull. Like the man, the house is an eclectic combination of unusual and familiar, flamboyant and sturdy.

Born in Bergen in 1810, the eldest of ten children raised in comfort, Bull began to show an interest in music at a very early age. When he was five he received his first violin and played well almost immediately. At eight he could play in string quartets at home, and by the time he was nine he had made his debut as a soloist. Bull veered away from formal studies as an adolescent and devoted his time to playing the violin. He was known to jump out the school window to take long walks in the woods with his instrument tucked under his arm. When his father sent him to college in Oslo in 1828, Bull failed his entrance examinations but prospered as a musician, becoming conductor of the city orchestra at age eighteen. At this time the spirit of patriotism was building in Norway as a show of defiance against the foreign rule that had dominated cultural life for hundreds of years, first under the Danes, then under the Swedes. The young Bull contributed to the swell of nationalism as it gripped his countrymen and eventually became a living symbol of the culture that Norway was determined to recapture

OPPOSITE: After performing around the world for forty-five years, violin virtuoso Ole Bull—the "Paganini of the North"—returned to his native Norway, where he had a summer villa built for his family on the island of Lysøen in 1872.

LEFT: Architect Conrad Fredrik van der Lippe incorporated elaborate Moorish tracery, arches, and spires with popular nineteenth-century Carpenter Gothic motifs. The villa was dubbed Little Alhambra, a reference to its Spanish influence.

ABOVE: Stenciled unfinished pine paneling warms an intimate bedroom.

OPPOSITE: An arched double window with a roundel illuminates a corner of the kitchen.

and glorify. Like the composer Jean Sibelius in Finland, Bull coupled great talent with an appreciation for his country's peasant past and folk music and thus was embraced by the common man and aficionado alike.

Ole Bull put Norway on the world map musically. In 1835, after a successful European tour, he was invited to perform solo at the Paris Opéra, an honor previously reserved only for Paganini, his idol. Thereafter he was received to great acclaim in concerts and at royal recitals throughout Europe and Russia, and on his first trip to the United States, in 1843, he was welcomed effusively. An audience gave him a standing ovation when he finished a concert on three strings after one snapped during the performance. He spiritedly incorporated "Yankee Doodle" into his repertoire to great peals of delight. On a Mississippi riverboat he knocked flat a ruffian who proposed to relieve him of his diamond-studded bow; the man was so impressed that he offered Bull his Bowie knife as a memento.

Touring internationally for forty-five years, Bull was a fiery performer and developed a reputation for his tall tales, extravagance, and charisma. He had a special affinity for America, where he attempted to found a Norwegian colony in Pennsylvania in 1852. Always grandiose in his visions, Bull was not equally expert as a financial planner, and his experiment failed. Among his accomplishments, however, were the establishment of the first national theater in Norway and the discovery of the musical talents of young Edvard Grieg. He befriended Franz Liszt, one year his junior, with whom he performed in a very fashionable duet. On the occasion of his sixty-sixth birthday, he played his violin from the top of the great pyramid of Cheops because of a promise to the king of Sweden. He was the model for Henrik Ibsen's character Peer Gynt and a companion of Henry Wadsworth Longfellow, who created a character after him in *Tales of the Wayside Inn*.

In 1870, at age sixty, Bull married his second wife—a young American named Sara Thorp who was forty years his junior and the daughter of a senator and lumber tycoon from Wisconsin. She soon gave birth to a daughter, Olea, and each summer after touring, the Bull family returned to Norway for renewal and rest. Bull purchased a 175-acre island south of Bergen called Lysøen, and in 1872 he decided to build a villa there. Architect Conrad Fredrik van der Lippe translated the musician's fantastic visions derived from his extensive travels into a "little Alhambra" that encompassed traditional Norwegian forms and fanciful Moorish elements. Bull was an active participant in the project, exploring the forested shores of Lysøen by rowboat, drawing his own maps, and making sketches for the paths, plantings, and drainage on his own. He had gazebos built and ordered that twenty miles of wooded paths be covered with white sand and

LEFT: Local craftsmen
executed the pierced-wood
Moorish arches and twisted
columns of the central music
room. Traditional Norwegian
furnishings are interspersed
with such European pieces
as the Bohemian glass
chandeliers.

seashells lest a guest should lose his way on misty days or dark nights.

The villa captures the exoticism of the eastern motifs that enchanted Bull and the Romanticism that swept the country in the second half of the nineteenth century. The house's intricately carved woodwork, although employed to give shape to the musician's worldly tastes, is also a splendid show of local wood-carving skills passed down since the Viking era. An onion dome rises to cap off a tower. Moorish arches and spires ornament a pair of verandas and dramatically frame the vista of the fjord and distant villages. Yet beneath the stylized tower and verandas is a wooden villa that is very much in the Norwegian country vernacular.

Inside the villa, the exquisite display of craftsmanship is indisputably in union with the architecture of the house. The focal point is a sixty-foot music room where elaborately carved columns of local pine lift a series of arches that support the vaulted ceiling. Three large glass chandeliers were imported from Bohemia to light the space, and above the fireplaces at either end tall mirrors were mounted to reflect the candles and the play of light in the arches. Despite its Eastern character, the room provides an unintrusive backdrop for the mix of European and American furnishings that the Bulls brought from their travels abroad.

The bedrooms of Bull and his wife adjoined the music room so that he could work late into the night. This was also the center of family life, where the couple would read, play cards, and perform together (she at the piano) for friends. It was in this room seven summers after their first season in the house that a much-weakened Bull rested, near death. A flotilla of ships paused beneath his window, and the military band struck up some of his best-loved tunes to salute him. And here his body was laid in state, in 1880, prior to one of the biggest funeral processions in Norway's history.

After Bull's death, Sara and his descendants continued to reside at Lysøen nearly every summer. The living and

ABOVE: Sylvea Bull's bedroom. The light-filled space, decorated by her mother, Olea, around 1905, uses the old Norwegian technique of rose painting.

OPPOSITE: A bath overlooks the wooded property.

dining rooms on the lower level were among those fully redecorated in 1905 when his daughter, Olea, made plans to move to the island from the United States. Those plans were never realized, however, because of her untimely death. Private rooms on the second floor were also expanded and refurbished over the years. A white bedroom was especially embellished for Olea's daughter, Sylvea, using the old Norwegian technique of rose painting.

It was Sylvea Bull Curtis who gave Lysøen to the Society for the Preservation of Norwegian Ancient Monuments in 1973. The villa is now open from mid-May to September and can be reached from a pier where a small boat ferries visitors over. Recitals are given in the music room each season, for which prominent guest artists are

invited to perform on Bull's eighteenth-century violin. Gazing up at the decorative arches while the sweetness of Bull's own violin resonates, one can imagine with what feeling the proud maestro might have played here in such a private moment as Sara recalls in her memoirs:

The music room, cheerful with wood fires and candles while the storm without promised seclusion, tempted him to do the best work into the night. When the fire and candles burned low, and the shadows seemed the intruding spirits of the storm, then the notes would be thrown aside, and that wonderful instrument, a soul in the hand of its master, would voice the tempest outside and the peace within.

Giorgio Armani

The Italian Designer's Cliffside
Villa on Antigua Reflects His Sleekly
Elegant Style

Text by Joseph Giovannini
Photography by Durston Saylor

Some travelers are simply peripatetic, but Giorgio Armani
is, more precisely, a peripatetic of the heliotropic variety:
He travels to find places with dependable sun. With seaside houses on the remote Italian island of Pantelleria
and a renovated farmhouse on the Tuscan coast—not
to mention a superyacht berthed in Saint-Tropez—the
couturier has most of his bases in the Mediterranean covered. But even in the Mediterranean the sun is iffy in
winter, and then Armani repairs to a retreat on the
Caribbean island of Antigua. He has arranged his life so
that the sun never really sets on his collection of retreats.

It might seem easier to follow the seasons of the sun
in seaside hotels, but Armani prefers to create paradisaical
worlds of his own, typified by visual quiet and the agree-
ment of all the parts, from the architecture down to stately
little table lamps and watermelon-red napkins. Famous
for unstructured tailoring, he designs environments that

For his dramatic cliffside
retreat on the Caribbean
island of Antigua, Giorgio
Armani brought his distinctive personal style to two
linked villas that celebrate
indoor-outdoor living. The
villas, which overlook Galley
Bay, follow the rocky contours down the cliff. Connected by a network of
terraces that offer both passage and refuge, the enclave
enfolds tropical gardens,
swimming pools, and a private beach.

ABOVE: In Villa Flower, bright
splashes of color punctuate
an otherwise dark-toned
dining area.

relax formality in favor of an elegant, easy simplicity. As on the body, so in the house.

Nature was showing off when it created Galley Bay, on the west coast of Antigua, whose rolling hills and craggy promontories rise up from gulfs of turquoise water lined with white beaches. Cloud formations regularly embellish the tableau, reproducing in the sky nebulous versions of the dramatic land formations.

Even Armani, a master of tonal nuance and shape, couldn't improve on nature's divine riff of color and form. "Antigua is quite simply one of the most scenic islands in the Caribbean, with lush areas of countryside juxtaposed against a myriad selection of beaches," says the designer. "Antiguans are the warmest, most welcoming hosts, who immediately make you feel at home."

Armani started with a pair of existing villas located on a promontory landscaped with a large tropical garden. When he travels, Armani acts as a paterfamilias, bringing along relatives and friends as houseguests on long sojourns. On Antigua, he needed to expand the villas into a complex that would retain a sense of domestic intimacy without looking like a boutique hotel.

Armani enlarged the compound by a simple process of addition and a deft touch of strategic reorganization. Each of the two structures, Villa Flower and Villa Serena, was designed in Antigua's vernacular style, with peaked, shingled roofs that act as parasols left open at the sides. He expanded the villas, each with several bedrooms, by

RIGHT: To accommodate family and friends, Armani (above right) added three guest pavilions to the existing villas, then joined them to the compound via pathways decked with cumaru wood. Steps descend to the entrance of Villa Flower, which has a cluster of peaked roofs that draw on Antiguan style.

linking them to satellite pavilions. A large, central living room at the core distributes guests to their respective villas and pavilions like a piazza within the house.

The pavilions, which step down the slopes, have verandas that overlook the view and lagoon, and windows throughout have louvers and mosquito netting rather than glass. "I wanted a real feeling of openness to the elements," Armani explains. Paths wind their way to beaches below the complex. The new village flows on its site as easily and inevitably as water down a hill.

It is not possible to compete successfully with the perfection of this postcard view, and Armani doesn't even try. By instinct, and as an Italian, Armani is a classicist, and in deference to the view, he quiets the interiors with all-natural materials and a palette of muted grays and beiges that avoid contrast in favor of the sense of harmony that he believes is the key to serenity. Floors and walls of the bedrooms and living rooms are clad in tatami, which he brings outside to the loggias. Wood runs through the interiors, and handsome cumaru planks, similar to teak, are used on all the stairs and decking.

Working on the interiors with his Armani Casa Interior Design Studio team, he borrowed heavily from his own line of furniture, Armani Casa. The sofas, chairs, tables, and even housewares blend a Japanese sense of simplicity with the feeling of repose often found in the roomy Art Deco furniture by Émile-Jacques Ruhlmann, an Armani inspiration.

As in his fashions, where the clothes don't wear the wearer, the furniture doesn't overwhelm the house: "The house must be lived," he has said. Designing for comfort and informality, Armani simply casts furniture in a supporting role, not as design divas demanding attention. The furniture, even long sofas made to measure, defer to rooms that themselves defer to nature's own masterpiece outside.

"In all of my homes, I am looking to create an ambience of sophisticated comfort that also reflects the spirit of the house's location," he says. "On the beach in Antigua, my aim has been to create an environment, both outside and inside, which harmonizes my aesthetic with the sensibilities of the West Indies."

RIGHT: To complement the grays of the interior, the exterior and linked balustrades of Villa Flower were painted charcoal.

Haga Pavilion

King Gustav III's Enchanted Realm Outside Stockholm

Text by Philip Mansel
Photography by José Luis Pérez

Gustav III, king of Sweden from 1771 to 1792, was one of the cleverest men who ever sat on a throne. He wrote operas and translated Voltaire with the same panache with which he defeated Catherine the Great of Russia and quelled disobedient Swedish nobles. He was a man of such refinement that in Sweden he is remembered as "the charmer king," and the word Gustavian is still a synonym for elegance. Haga Pavilion, set in a park on a lake outside Stockholm, is the finest memorial to King Gustav and his age. Like many royal buildings, it drew its inspiration from France.

When Gustav III visited France in 1784, the queen, Marie Antoinette, gave an entertainment in his honor one evening at the Petit Trianon. The women wore white, the men scarlet and gold, and night was turned into day by flares and candles in the gardens. Gustav III wrote, "It was a real enchantment . . . a truly Elysian fete," and the Petit Trianon inspired him to create his own paradise at Haga.

Haga Pavilion was constructed, around an earlier house, from 1787 to 1792. King Gustav, who was a great Francophile, built Haga with both Swedish and French features. The architect was a Swede, Olof Tempelman; the decorator was a Frenchman, Louis Masreliez. Gustav III was the guiding force for much of the design. His notes can be seen on many of the plans, and he drew detailed sketches to show what he wanted.

Masreliez, who had traveled to Italy with the king, was inspired by Raphael's decoration in the Vatican and Piranesi's wild Neoclassical design, as well as by the ruins

OPPOSITE: In the King's Bed-chamber, a painting of Henry IV of France by Alexander Roslin represents a monarch greatly admired by Gustav III, who, like him, was to be assassinated.

LEFT: King Gustav III's beloved Haga Pavilion in Stockholm—completed in 1792, the year of his death—was designed by Olof Tempelman and modeled on the Petit Trianon at Versailles. It has been fully restored.

OPPOSITE: The interiors were done by Louis Masreliez, who brought the Pompeian style to Sweden. A marble bust commands the dining room, which leads to the drawing room.

ABOVE: The library's fireplace is from a Piranesi design; above it is a cast of Sergel's medallion of Swedish ambassador to France, poet and collector Count Creutz, from whom Gustav III acquired his book collection. The king's son, Adolf, removed the books and took them to Germany when he was exiled in 1809; they were brought back in the 1920s. Of the original furniture, only the library steps and chair survive.

of Pompeii. The interior of Haga is in the late-Gustavian style, which is a deliberate rejection of the Rococo. The thirteen rooms are decorated in colors that are purer and cooler than contemporary French taste. Indeed, when he went shopping in Paris, Gustav III often said, "That decoration is too elaborate; it is suitable for the queen. I want something more simple."

Haga shows what France missed by turning its energies from the art of living to the practice of revolution after 1789. It is so alive, so representative of Gustav III and his style, that around every corner one expects to see the fascinating, electric figure of the king wearing the black-and-red Swedish national costume, which he designed himself.

Haga was repeatedly altered and painted over during the nineteenth century. However, with the help of 153 original drawings by Masreliez, and surviving inventories and receipts, it was restored to a close approximation of its former state between 1937 and 1948.

One of the charms of Haga is that it blends perfectly into the surrounding landscape. That is hardly surprising,

since its English-style park was designed by the king's friend Fredrik Magnus Piper, "Surveyor to the Royal Household." The king had sent him to England to study gardens, and Piper believed that a park should resemble "beauteous Nature [so] that the most initiated will never discern any trace of the artifice and expense devoted to them." Set on the edge of one of Stockholm's innumerable lakes, Haga Park contains characteristic eighteenth-century ornaments: Turkish copper "tents" at the entrance, a Turkish kiosk, a Chinese pavilion, a temple where the king could eat in the summer, and an orangery.

Gustav III did not enjoy Haga for long. In 1789, with the support of the poor and the peasants, he carried out a second bloodless coup d'état against the powerful and corrupt Swedish aristocracy. They were enraged by their loss of power, by the king's extravagance and constant wars, and by his handsome young favorite, Count Armfelt. In 1792, although running out of money—the royal household could not pay its bills—Gustav III was nonetheless thinking of another war to free Louis XVI

RIGHT: The walls of the drawing rooms, which are decorated with paintings of the deities Juno, Apollo, Jupiter, and Minerva, are testimony to Masreliez's years of study in Italy. The furniture is Swedish, by Erik Öhrmark, except for the mahogany *console desserte*, which was fashioned by Adam Weisweiler.

and Marie Antoinette from the control of the revolutionaries in Paris.

A group of aristocratic conspirators decided that assassination was the only solution. The king, who was spending more and more time away from Stockholm at Haga, received many warnings. Indeed, one night two conspirators, Anckarström and Horn, crept up to Haga under cover of darkness to murder the king. However, they were so terrified by seeing him through the tall ground-floor windows, lying on a sofa surrounded by his books, that they ran away.

On his last day at Haga, March 16, 1792, Gustav III inspected progress on the palace that he had started to build on a hill above the pavilion, watched sleighs racing on the lake, and then drove by sleigh himself over the snow to Stockholm to attend the last masked ball of the season in the opera house. During a quadrille in the middle of the ball he was shot in the back by Anckarström. He died, after immense suffering, thirteen days later. The king's end has been immortalized in words and music in one of Verdi's greatest operas, *Un Ballo in Maschera*. Haga Pavilion immortalized the king in wood and stone.

ABOVE: A series of arched French windows distinguishes the dining room, which forms a large part of the north wing. The chairs are a Swedish interpretation of a Chippendale design and are signed by Öhrmark. The console tables were designed by Masreliez; the sideboards were designed by L. J. Desprez.

ABOVE: Built to open onto and reflect the surrounding landscape, the Mirror Room creates for visitors the illusion that they are floating on a lake. Its classical character is enhanced by the decoration in the style of Robert Adam and the friezes above the columns that depict Apollo, Minerva, Homer, and Virgil. The pine floors were painted to look like mahogany. The sofa and chairs were modeled after ancient Klismos designs.

RIGHT: Turkish-style copper "tents" stand guard at the entrance to Haga Park.

A Kenyan Sanctuary

Dodo and Michael Cunningham-Reid's Tower on Lake Naivasha

Text by Elizabeth Lambert
Photography by Jonathan Pilkington

OPPOSITE: To create a game sanctuary, Dodo and Michael Cunningham-Reid bought five hundred acres of land on Lake Naivasha in Kenya and began construction of a tower as a weekend retreat. "The most important person on the project was the engineer, Nick Evans. He's a genius," says Dodo, who conceived the pagoda-like eight-story structure. "Concrete was used for the first three floors, then a steel rib cage clad in Kenyan cypress. There's a lot of high tech in there, but you can't see it."

RIGHT: Clouds form over Lake Naivasha, which draws a wide range of wildlife, including cheetahs and giraffes.

At night hippos graze at the base of the tower, and from a balcony, their munching and chortling sound like old men laughing. If there is a full moon, the colobus monkeys are peaceful. If there is a cheetah in the neighborhood, they take to raucous whooping. Giraffes, impalas and zebras are quieter visitors, but in the morning it is the cry of the fish eagle that reverberates along the shore of Lake Naivasha, Kenya.

This is where Michael and Dodo Cunningham-Reid are creating a sanctuary for the animals and living among them in the tower they have built as a weekend house. It is land that once belonged to Michael's stepfather, Tom, Lord Delamere, and he knew it well as a young man, so it is "a source of great satisfaction to have been able to buy five hundred acres back, to have a presence on Lake Naivasha again," he says.

The tower grew from Dodo's determination to create "something artistic" in Africa, and she intends it as a symbol. "The continent is dominated by war, poverty, despair," she says. "I had been lobbying against so many things and realized that I couldn't change matters, but I still needed to do something, so I built a tower as a symbol of peace and hope. Some people paint a picture or write a poem when they have a certain mood. I built a tower.

"It began as a dream, but the form of it came into my head one morning, so I scribbled it out and took that drawing to an architect who could base it in reality. I suppose there are Nordic influences because I was born in Germany, but the design is not based on any academic study of architecture. It's what was there when I drew it out. What I do is emotional, not rational."

OPPOSITE: The living room on the second floor, with an adjoining library, has native mahogany for the paneling and mantel. "Everything had to be treated for insects, of course," says Dodo. "You name it, we've got it."

ABOVE: Most of the antiques, including the living room's Gothic Revival table, at right, came from the English estate of Mary, Lady Delamere, Michael's mother. "I'm not an expert on birds, but the fish eagle is what Lake Naivasha is famous for," says Dodo. "We have binoculars and bird books at the tower, so I'm learning."

Her husband, knowing just how difficult it is to build anything at Lake Naivasha, much less a complicated tower, thought she was crazy but knew she was determined, so he gave the go-ahead.

And so the tower was built. Curious monkeys watched as it grew taller and joined their territory in the tops of the yellow fever trees. Birds nested in the steel rib cage. Construction took four years, but she was not in a hurry. Then, there it was, looking from across the lake like a delicately carved wood toy.

"You are not aware of its size until you are closer to it," she says, "and then it molds to its surroundings, par-ticularly in the morning and evening light, when the wood is the same color as the trees and the tower looks like another tree trunk. When the wind blows, the top sways slightly, in rhythm with the trees. That swaying is an essential engineering tolerance, but it becomes poetry. I do see the tower as a tree, and when friends are sitting out on the balconies, they look to me like leopards who have gone up into the branches to rest."

But if it is a tree, it is an octagonal one. "To create the rooms, I divided each of the eight levels like cake slices. The living room is three large cake slices wide, the small-est bedroom is only one." She buys furniture whenever

they are in London, and a friend in France keeps an eye out for antique fabrics and furniture. "That is a great help," she says. "I hate shopping." But finding things was easy compared with all the crating and shipping, then hoisting everything up into the tower on ropes slung over balcony railings.

Furnishings from Nairobi include dining chairs copied from a book of Biedermeier furniture. "I wanted to give them some edge, otherwise they would be too serious, so I covered the seats with handwoven checked fabric from Nairobi and had them deeply buttoned, like Victorian furniture," she explains.

There is a tranquillity that floats over the tower, which is topped with a meditation room. "Friends arrive," she says, "perhaps from frustrating lives, perhaps with the dust of a safari still on them, and find themselves in the Garden of Eden. This is a sanctuary for more than just the animals. One visitor arrived and couldn't speak for an hour. Another was silent when we went out in the evening and returned to find the tower completely hidden in mist. Finally, she said that she had thought this might be a fairy tale but now knew it to be true. 'The tower is there,' she said, 'but it will only be found by those who are meant to find it.'"

Pride and Preservation

The Duke and Duchess of Northumberland Update England's Storied Alnwick Castle

Text by Elizabeth Lambert
Photography by Andrew Twort

"We couldn't just move into a castle and expect the children to be grateful," says Jane Percy, the Duchess of Northumberland. "This place was not designed for kids."

Several years ago her husband, Ralph, the twelfth Duke of Northumberland, inherited the vast estate at Alnwick and its castle, which was built by Normans in the eleventh century and enlarged with towers and gatehouses by the Percy family in the fourteenth century. The Percys ruled Northumberland from these stone walls.

In peaceful times the family turned from war to comforts and created rooms that speak of a different kind of power. Robert Adam designed new state rooms in the eighteenth century; the fourth duke took out those rooms in the nineteenth century and imported skilled Italian artisans by the boatload to create new ones that rank among the best Victorian decoration in the country.

Today, Alnwick is second only to Windsor as the largest inhabited castle in England. The paintings and porcelain are world famous, and the architecture is so evocative that it was used as a setting for Hogwarts School in the first two Harry Potter films.

"How do you make four children feel at home with all that?" says the duchess. "But there was no choice. If we didn't live here, the castle would just become a museum."

RIGHT: Ralph and Jane Percy, the Duke and Duchess of Northumberland, have renovated several state rooms and private quarters at Alnwick Castle, their eleventh-century estate in England. The six-thousand-acre property includes a water garden designed by landscape architects Jacques and Peter Wirtz.

OPPOSITE: "My job was to bring the room down a bit so people could live in it," designer Robert Kime says of the library, which he helped refurbish. Art, music, and science trophies adorn the coffered ceiling. Kime designed the fabric on the circa 1823 Morel and Hughes gilt armchairs.

Robert Kime, a designer with a deep understanding of great country houses, agreed completely. "Unless rooms are used, you can't make the house hum," he says. "The difficulty at Alnwick is that the wonderful suites of rooms go in circles. On every floor, corridors and rooms go round and round the castle."

The duchess had the solution. The state rooms are on two levels; the family would live below and above. She found small rooms tucked between massive stone walls and opened them up. She told the estate carpenters exactly what she wanted, and they built it using oak grown on the property. The family had a kitchen, a dining room, a living room, and a billiards room, a base where they could hope to find each other in all that vastness.

Bedrooms would have to be two floors up. At night they climb the Grand Staircase, past dark and empty state rooms, to go to bed. The children counted the stone stairs. There are one hundred and eleven. They got used to it.

Some of the bedrooms had been lived in by previous generations and needed cheering up. Some had been used as prisons for Cromwell's soldiers and needed a lot of cheering up. Vivien Greenock, then of Colefax and

ABOVE LEFT: "We were reluctant to move into a vast castle with all its treasures. These rooms make it possible to live a normal life," says the duchess. Covering the Georgian wing chair is *Marrakech Stripe*, one of several handwoven silk fabrics Kime has designed.

ABOVE: The Grand Staircase leads to the Upper Guard Chamber. Stuccowork, conceived by Italian decorative designer Giovanni Montiroli in the nineteenth century, ornaments the groin-vaulted ceiling. *Faux-marbre* panels painted by Charles Hesp are on the walls of the lower landing.

LEFT: "It provides a total contrast to the grandeur of the state rooms. It's a place to cook, eat, and relax," the duchess says of the kitchen in Prudhoe Tower, which she designed along with the family rooms. "Wall plaster was removed to reveal the nineteenth-century stonework."

Fowler, designed them all and installed baths. "Like all these houses, it had bedrooms by the dozen but almost no plumbing within a mile," she says.

Charles Hesp, an expert in paint effects, restored a mural that had been painted by the duke's grandmother and her daughters—"a pretty bit of chinoiserie," he says, "but it ended halfway up the wall in a straight line and looked as though a hedge cutter had roared through the room. We lengthened some branches and added birds and butterflies."

The Grand Staircase was another problem. It had rich panels of porphyry and white and Siena marbles, but the lower landing had blank white walls. Experts on historic design suggested that they paint them with distemper. "With six dogs wagging wet tails up those stairs every day?" says the duchess. "Not a good idea. It was Charles Hesp's idea to paint *faux-marbre* panels."

Today, the real and the painted panels are side by side, and nobody notices the difference. "If people walk past and don't notice my work, then it must be right," he says.

Kime advised on the state rooms, particularly the library, a room he considers to be, without doubt, "the greatest room in England." "My task was to make a large family room a comfortable place to read the newspaper but not disturb the splendor. Anything added had to be pretty strong to hold its own, so I designed a bold striped silk to cover a very good Georgian wing chair and another red-and-gold fabric for the Regency armchairs.

"Basically, I'm a maintenance man. What I love is reorganizing a house, helping owners to understand what they have inherited. A bed had been painted black, probably by the fourth duke in mourning, and looked like something of little value, a prime target for a clear-out." Kime's advice was, "I think I would wait if I were you." They did. His workshops chipped off the black paint by hand, and there was the original decoration, almost certainly by Adam.

"It can be confusing," he explains. "Furniture was often moved and spares banished to storage. All that surplus, dozens of identical chairs—it's tempting to sell a few. I was the restraining hand, keeping a suite of twenty-four chairs by the Regency designers Morel and Hughes intact. These ducal houses, where everything was looked after and cherished, are extraordinary. Alnwick is in the top league."

Kime feels strongly about honoring the possessions of a stately home. Show him to the attics, and he's like a terrier on the loose, persevering until he has investigated the treasures in every chest.

He found yellow silk draperies, carefully folded and put away by the duke's grandmother when war broke out. A note was enclosed to explain where they had hung. They are back in place. He found some Mughal fabric with twinkly silver embroidery on silk. That hangs on the Adam bed.

The castle is largely in order now, well loved and well used. The state rooms are open to the public for six months a year; the rest of the time they are used by the family. Life not only continues in the castle, it is geared up a notch with the excitement of the magnificent water garden the duchess and landscape architects Jacques and Peter Wirtz have created. Her fund-raising continues for phase two.

Alnwick is, as she says, "a castle on the outside, but inside we can feel as though we're living in a house."

LEFT: Portraits of the duke's ancestors hang in the State Dining Room. At rear is one of the fourth duke, who renovated the castle in the mid-1800s. The chairs are from Stanwick Hall, the Percy family seat. Estate craftsmen decorated the ceiling and carved the frames.

ABOVE: A chinoiserie mural painted by the duke's grandmother, the eighth duchess, and her daughters, Lady Elizabeth and Lady Diana, highlights a guest room. Hesp restored the mural and added taller branches, birds, and butterflies. The silk bedcovering is antique.

RIGHT: "I believe it was designed by Robert Adam," Kime says of the bed in a guest room. "We brought back the original colors, which we discovered underneath a black overpaint that had been applied in the nineteenth century, presumably during a mourning period for a duke."

Out of the Blue

On the Eastern Shore of Lake Michigan, a Home Is Memorably Shaped by Color and Geometry

Architecture by Margaret McCurry, FAIA, of Tigerman McCurry Architects
Text by Jeff Turrentine
Photography by Steve Hall/Hedrich Blessing

It's called Harbor Country now—a trademarked appellation coined nearly thirty years ago by boosters who envisioned their picturesque sliver of land, only sixty minutes from Chicago, as a future vacation home haven. Their work paid off, their hopes came true, and the term caught on. But architect Margaret McCurry, a native Chicagoan, recalls a time when the string of quiet, family-friendly communities along Lake Michigan didn't have a marketing plan. "Back then," she says, "this part of southwest Michigan was just called Southwest Michigan."

With her husband, Stanley Tigerman, McCurry is a principal of Tigerman McCurry Architects and a bona fide member of architectural royalty in Chicago, a city so justifiably proud of its design history that it named a downtown street after Mies van der Rohe. But she also has roots in this tiny corner of Michigan, near the Indiana state line, where she and Tigerman have maintained a home for many years. She first began building here—for friends, and then later for friends of friends, as word spread—twenty years ago; now she can't take a leisurely drive through the wooded lanes of Harbor Country without frequently passing one of her creations.

One of them, a lakeside getaway for a young family, isn't too hard to spot: It's the only three-and-a-half-story, metal-roofed, sapphire-blue house on the block. McCurry's clients wanted to make a bold chromatic statement; when she showed them a nearby house she'd built, whose tongue-and-groove cedar siding was painted a bright lipstick red, they loved what they saw. But copying the color would have been a faux pas. "That pretty much left yellow and blue," says McCurry.

Blue it was, and blue it is: a shade that celebrates the joyous meeting of lake and sky. This is a house that encourages—one might even say insists upon—engagement with its environment, thanks to a profusion of windows and glass doors that soak practically every square inch of the interior in light and allow for fantastic views, not only of the lake but also of the Galien River, which feeds into it, and the surrounding protected wetlands.

LEFT: The second-story deck of a residence designed by Margaret McCurry, of the Chicago-based firm Tigerman McCurry Architects.

OPPOSITE: "The small, upper-story windows create a wavelike pattern as they flow across the façade," says McCurry. She uses nautical imagery in describing the house, which "sports a continuous white-railed 'widow's walk' across its second story." The bedroom doors open onto the balcony, offering access to the "ship's rail."

OPPOSITE: In the living room, a balcony on the left, patio access on the right, and windows along the rear wall create an immediate connection to the outdoors. The goal was to "emphasize simple, relaxed relationships of public spaces with balanced, light-filled views," notes McCurry.

RIGHT: In the kitchen, a cooking island doubles as a counter for casual dining and socializing.

RIGHT: The sunroom is an ideal space to enjoy a panoramic sunset over the lake. An antique surveyor's stand forms the base of the floor lamp.

The views inside are impressive, too. McCurry—who majored in art history at Vassar before becoming an architect—knows how to achieve dramatic effects by framing her spaces, forcing the eye to take in various elements one at a time rather than all at once. A visitor entering from the front door, for example, looks up a small flight of stairs and sees, at eye level, the dining table, which sits at the intersection of the house's north-south and east-west axes; the image is cropped tight so that one has no choice but to regard it independently before ascending the stairs and situating the dining area in the context of the larger axial plan.

McCurry takes great pride in providing what she calls "little encounters, little surprises," and here they abound. There probably aren't many houses, for instance, where a dinner guest would be happy to spend the entire meal staring at the underside of a staircase; in McCurry's hands, however, it becomes a bold architectural element, hovering over the space between the entrance hall and the dining area, every bit as hypnotizing as a Donald Judd

sculpture. Or consider the way she turns an ordinary walk up a flight of stairs into a mini-event, with clever window placement that creates an atrium-like effect in the main stairwell and gives brief, tantalizing glimpses into other rooms. When was the last time architecture inspired you to pause, appreciatively, along a staircase?

If this house could be said to have a unifying geometric element, it would have to be a grid. Small, square windows—which have become a sort of McCurry signature—pop up regularly on all the floors. "Often we'll use square windows without muntins, and if you pile up a bunch of them, it gives you the effect of a single oversize muntin—so you get a kind of modern version of the old-fashioned window grid," she says.

On the second floor, a master suite and a pair of children's bedrooms open to a lake-facing deck that runs the full length of the house. The rooms are simply designed and just as simply decorated; these are spaces for relaxing after a long summer's day spent walking along the dunes or wading in the gently lapping waves. But just above this

ABOVE: Crisp colors in the master bedroom reflect the hues of the lake and the surrounding woods. The balcony and deck are shared by the two children's rooms.

floor is yet another surprise: The attic isn't an attic at all, but a loftlike wing containing two guest rooms and a media room. The clients' young children—and anyone with a childlike love of small, cubbyhole spaces—can't help but thrill over the unique touches McCurry has added up here, including a string of knee-level windows just below the eaves and a pair of tiny window seats, the perfect spot for a child's afternoon nap.

Though she's filled this house with delightful details, McCurry has also made sure to instill it with the logic that is fundamental to her ethos. "Axiality is a very important part of my work," she says. "I want it to be the case that you can always sense where you're going when you walk down the stairs or turn a corner. It creates a sense of calm. But I also like to play with it—just a little."

Tropical Infusion

A Florida House Vividly Joins Cultures and Collections

Architecture and Interior Design by
Peter Marino, AIA
Text by Joseph Giovannini
Photography by Scott Frances

Uneasy may be the head that wears the crown. But in a Palm Beach collection of Southeast Asian sculpture, tiaras of standing cobras arrayed on the heads of divinities give ample reason for the assurance behind their beatific smiles. New York architect Peter Marino, however, has taken his own measures to secure the serenity of these elevated beings. The ancient figures may now find themselves relocated to Palm Beach, but the house Marino designed for a New York couple, a series of pavilions ringing a long grassy courtyard landscaped with tropical plants and trees, was influenced by the architecture of Southeast Asia and its lush environment. "The collection inspired us to do something different, and this, after all, is the tropics," says the wife. "The statues were born in a place like this, and they've returned to their setting."

The seeds of the twenty-thousand-square-foot house that overlooks the Atlantic were planted in the early 1980s, as the couple, who had a winter house on the island, started collecting Southeast Asian art. When they eventually decided to trade their western view, with its punishing afternoon sun, for the gentler morning light of

A couple's collection of Southeast Asian art was the starting point for an ocean-front Palm Beach house designed by Peter Marino. RIGHT: A Lalanne chandelier in the dining pavilion hangs above Kaare Klint–designed chairs. Japanese split-bamboo blinds afford partial views of the front courtyard and a lotus pond. "The dark space highlights the exterior both during the day and night," Marino explains.

the eastern shore, they hired Marino, who proposed building the new house around the growing collection. "Why not create an Asian environment throughout?" he recalls thinking. "It could be the stock that binds the soup. The idiom suited the art."

Marino, who trained as a modernist, takes his cues from the particulars of a site, client, and commission. Designing in the tropics of Florida, where pastels have become the de facto state colors, Marino decided, counterintuitively, to build a house in a palette of dark woods. "You feel cool in dark spaces," he says.

In the context of Palm Beach, where architectural review boards favor traditional designs, Marino sought roots appropriate for the climate. Traditional buildings in Southeast Asia, with high hip roofs, act as parasols against the beating sun; long overhangs cut glare. The pavilions Marino proposed agreed both with the clients' collections and with the reality of Florida weather.

The magic starts as the driveway, paved with volcanic stone, curves like a question mark into the estate. Marino obscures any trace of the outside world: "I wanted hyperdense vegetation so you'd discover the house, as though coming across it in a jungle," he says. "You don't see the

whole house at any one time." Florida itself, virtually a greenhouse, provided the opportunity to transplant mature tropical trees, and the new garden is already seasoned enough to lure small squadrons of dragonflies: Marino's landscape has quickly become an ecosystem.

Symmetrical flights of stairs rise from the driveway up a half level to a grassy plinth that forms the courtyard within a compound of buildings, each with a distinctive roof. Marino and his associates imported from Indonesia all the roof tiles and wood (*merbau*), most of which was cut and crafted before being shipped in containers. A pagoda draped in bolts of saffron and yellow textiles presides at one end of a black-bottomed pool set on axis with a lotus pond just outside the dining pavilion. The high and low roofscapes reflect the hierarchy of pavilions that compose the ensemble.

Bronze front doors open to a monumentally tall entrance hall with a framed view of the ocean, seen across a lawn trimmed like a putting green. A heroically tall stone statue explains the thirty-five-foot apex of the room. Keeping the visual thermometer down, Marino applied dark green lacquer to the walls, using a classic Asian technique, and he deepened the shadows created by the roof

BELOW: In the paneled library, Fernand Léger's 1954 canvas, *Les Campeurs,* hangs above the mantel; displayed on the easel is a work by El Lissitzky.

ABOVE: Marino wanted to give the impression of a house in the jungle, "with all the mature plantings," he says.

overhangs by bringing the *merbau* inside. The floors and ceilings throughout the house are surfaced in the dark wood. "I couldn't easily get the wide planks and the feeling of a Southeast Asian forest from an American tree," he explains.

If he veils the house outside with plants, he mystifies the interiors by building up shadows. Standing on pedestals, along axes that tie the pavilions together, the Southeast Asian figures seem to linger in the depths of an ambiguous time. "The house has a peaceful feeling," confirms the wife.

The shadows smooth transitions, pairing the ancient sculptures with another collection, classic modern pieces from the early twentieth century. All the artworks, which include several by German Expressionists—among them, Ernst Ludwig Kirchner—and paintings by El Lissitzky and Man Ray, are museum caliber, but rather than isolating them under cones of light in white rooms, Marino conjures an aura that binds them, creating a domestic environment in which the art forms part of a complex

whole. The atmosphere bridges the gaps between millennia and cultures, bringing the unusual, even unlikely, combinations together seamlessly. "I strive for an integration that enhances each object," says Marino.

If the sculpture finds a context in the house and setting, the paintings find a context with furniture from the 1920s and 1930s, mostly by French masters, including Jean-Michel Frank, Eugène Printz, Émile-Jacques Ruhlmann, Paul Dupré-Lafon, and Pierre Chareau. Opening the bottom drawer of an impressive Ruhlmann cabinet in the master bedroom, the wife points out the extraordinary woods of the interior, exhibiting an intimate knowledge of the details. Passionate collectors, she and her husband maintain a reference library on the works they acquire.

Just as his Palm Beach clients collect with a depth of knowledge fed by the tomes on their bookshelves, Marino and his associates are scholars of both design and architectural history. "Frank de Biasi, who worked on the

ABOVE: A stone figure is displayed in the dining pavilion.

interior design, was at Christie's, and the head of the Paris office, Gay Gassmann, who helped locate important decorative objects and furniture, worked at the J. Paul Getty Museum," Marino explains. Assisted with the house's architecture by senior associate George Restrepo, Marino is one of the few architects who offer designs integrated from structure to furniture and practice across centuries and continents with remarkable fluency and expertise.

While Marino established the floors and ceilings as a visual through line in all the rooms, he created a secondary datum with the furniture, much of it low and massive, anchoring the rooms in comfort. He upholstered the pieces within the groupings in different fabrics but limited their tonal range to guarantee unity within the diversity. In a signature move, he boldly used plaid draperies and striped carpets to throw unexpected patterns into the subdued mix. He often used exotic fabrics, such as the colorful antique phulkari bedcovering in the master bedroom. "I came to architecture from painting," he says. "I feel I'm creating three-dimensional paintings."

Marino further edged the interiors toward art by commissioning artists to do one-of-a-kind pieces. The French sculptor Claude Lalanne executed a fairy-tale chandelier of branching limbs for the dining room, plus bronze settees teeming with elephantine ginkgo leaves and rampant salamanders looking as though they just fell out of a jungle scene by Rousseau. French artist Robert Goossens fashioned a pair of mock-Baroque mirrors for the room, in an elegant sendup of tradition. Everywhere the craftsmanship is refined. Stamped- and silvered-leather wallcoverings and a hand-tufted silk carpet shimmer together in a powder room. Walls in the master bedroom are hand-plastered with incised swirls that recall Matisse's floral cutouts.

Nowhere in this complex house layered in different times and cultures is there a lapse in tone. No discordant detail pierces the aura or breaks the perfection. Marino and his clients have brought architecture, landscape, art, and furniture together in an exceptional *Gesamtkunstwerk* that emerged through a collaboration of venturesome connoisseurs.

BELOW: The master bedroom
is situated in a corner of
the house. One of a pair of
Chareau tub chairs is near
an Émile-Jacques Ruhlmann
cabinet.

President and Mrs. Ronald Reagan's White House

Text by Russell Lynes and Sam Burchell
Photography by Derry Moore

Unlike the residences of chiefs of state in almost every other great nation, the White House, in Washington, D.C., is a home, not a palace. Though not large, by any standards it is a distinguished building, and for almost two hundred years it has been the symbol of American democracy and of the American presidency. The formal rooms on the first two floors are visited by more than a million and a half people a year, and it is, of course, the setting for state occasions and receptions and for much of the business of government. Nevertheless, for all the pomp and circumstance, there is a comforting continuity evident. For here is "The President's House," and white match folders proclaim the fact. So it has been since the day President and Mrs. John Adams moved into the private part of the White House, in 1800—an American heritage and a home.

Every First Family puts their own stamp on the residence, and President and Mrs. Ronald Reagan were no exception, redecorating the second and third floors of the building, the area that included their private apartments, and other rooms, among them the Yellow Oval Room, the Treaty Room, the Lincoln Bedroom, and the Queen's Bedroom. With tact and discernment, Mrs. Reagan made certain that this was, for the term of office, the president's private home and her own. To achieve this end, the first lady enlisted the aid of Los Angeles interior designer Ted Graber, an old family friend, who had long been familiar with President and Mrs. Reagan's tastes and preferences.

At the beginning, of course, there was a great deal of work necessary. Graber was proud of the fact that "on Inauguration Day, when President and Mrs. Reagan arrived at the White House at five o'clock, the sitting room at the west end of the second floor was complete, filled with their furniture and personal possessions brought from California." However, as the designer explained, the real work of refurbishing the private apartments did not begin until January 21, 1981. As Mrs. Reagan and her designer well knew, there is far more to a house than furniture and paintings and possessions. "We wanted it to be warm and livable," said Graber, "without sacrificing

OPPOSITE: Resplendent with double-arched windows, the West Sitting Hall served as President and Mrs. Reagan's second floor living room. Furnishings from their California residence were installed on Inauguration Day; the room was later painted and given new draperies and carpeting.

Working with interior designer Ted Graber, President and Mrs. Ronald Reagan refurbished the private apartments of the White House, as well as certain other rooms on the second and third floors, using much of the White House collection. LEFT: The north façade.

OPPOSITE: Mrs. Reagan and Graber rearranged the second floor Yellow Oval Room to make it more comfortable for heads of state who gathered there to converse and exchange official gifts before state dinners. The sofas and the gilt-base marble-top tables were added to the formal setting. Flanking the chimneypiece were American paintings: at left, by Thomas Moran (top) and David Kennedy; at right, by Childe Hassam (top) and Andrew Melrose. A canvas by Jasper F. Cropsey adorned the overmantel. Eighteenth-century French furniture included a *bureau plat*, bronze gueridon tables, and gilded fauteuils stamped *C. Sené*.

RIGHT: The President's Study, on the second floor, was filled with the first family's own furniture, augmented by antiques and paintings from the White House collection. A favorite among the personal effects on President Reagan's mahogany partners desk was a silver repoussé fire chief's horn made into a lamp base, given to the president when he was governor of California. Pre-Columbian sculptures from the president's own collection rested on the marble mantel, and on either side of *Boy Fishing*, by Lilla Cabot Perry, were paintings of American Indian subjects by George Catlin, on loan from the National Gallery of Art.

any of the historical traditions." Most important was the atmosphere—one that was pleasant and welcoming.

This was readily apparent in President Reagan's study on the second floor, where the formality of the Oval Office was set aside. It was a personal room, filled with photographs and mementos—a room of dignity and ease. The desk was his own; on it was a splendid mid-nineteenth-century silver repoussé fire chief's horn, made into a lamp, a gift from a friend when Reagan was governor of California. The paintings of American Indians, by George Catlin, brought to mind a statement by noted horticulturist and writer A. J. Downing, who had such an extensive influence on the American home in the 1840s and who landscaped the White House grounds in 1850. "Much of the character of everyman," he wrote, "may be read in his house." Surely this statement reinforced the personal atmosphere that existed in the White House. Pri-

vate though the first family's living quarters may have been, however, the rooms belonged to the American people. For example, the Catlins on the wall of the president's study, six of them from the National Gallery of Art, might well have been known to President Andrew Jackson—though President Jackson's "West" was a very different place from President Reagan's. It is just such a sense of history and continuity that informs even the private presidential portions of the executive mansion.

When Mrs. Reagan and Graber set out to bring renewed life to the second and third floors of the White House, they had remarkable spaces and architectural details with which to work. Thanks to a previous first lady, Mrs. Coolidge, what was once a shallow attic had been transformed into a pleasant third floor. Here there are guest rooms, sitting rooms, an informal hall, and, up a walkway leading to the surface over the South Portico,

a solarium. The room is an octagon, flooded with light, and Mrs. Coolidge herself called it "the sky parlor." The view from the wide windows is over treetops and across the broad South Lawn to the Washington and Jefferson monuments. As a result of the joint efforts of Mrs. Reagan and Graber, the space invited leisure with informal sofas and chairs covered in a colorful floral fabric. Clearly, the room was designed with comfort and ease in mind. This point of view was characteristic of even the more formal rooms in the private White House apartments. To one degree or another, all of the rooms were quite as gracious, cheerful, and restful.

Naturally, the White House—since 1792, when James Hoban won the competition to design it—has gone through a number of renovations and reconstructions and redecorations, not to mention two fires. Indeed, the house was still unfinished when President and Mrs. Adams moved in. The main staircase had not been completed; the wood-burning fireplaces could not subdue the cold and damp; bells to summon staff had not been installed, and there was no laundry yard. "The great unfinished audience room," Mrs. Adams wrote her daughter, "I made a drying room of." In 1801, when President Jefferson moved in, roofs leaked and plaster was falling from the ceilings, and he called upon architect Benjamin Henry Latrobe to come to the rescue. The greatest devastation came, of course, in 1814, when President James Madison and his wife, Dolley, were the occupants of the White House, and British troops put it to the torch. The house had recently been redecorated by Mrs. Madison, with the imaginative advice of Latrobe, and all their work went up in smoke. However, as the British troops were approaching, Mrs. Madison managed to take "nearly all" of the silver, the velvet curtains, and the Gilbert Stuart portrait of George Washington—now in the East Room—out of harm's way.

Since Latrobe's day, there have been numerous structural changes in the President's House, as it was once called, most of them externally invisible. At the urging of President Theodore Roosevelt, the Congress appropriated funds to redo walls and reinforce the underpinnings of the house with steel and concrete. Later, President Coolidge found that President Roosevelt's attempts to strengthen the structure had been a good deal less than satisfactory. And so it went, until President Truman finally faced up to a century and a half of gradual decay and unsuccessful renovations and to the literal threat of collapse. The day he saw the chandelier in the East Room sway as a color guard walked on the floor above, and when he felt the floor of his study trembling, he took action. Congress approved a generous budget, and a complete renovation of the building took place from 1949 to 1952. If by standards of exact historical preservation the White House today is less than perfect, it is now solid and supported entirely by steel.

President and Mrs. Reagan did not face as many architectural renovations as had confronted some of their predecessors; they were able to concentrate their efforts on refurbishing primarily the private areas of the White House and restoring much of its antique furniture collection. Excellent use was made of the precedent established by Mrs. Coolidge, who successfully undertook to persuade Congress "to authorize the acceptance of appropriate antiques as gifts." Mrs. John F. Kennedy, as well, mounted a campaign to attract gifts of furniture and works of art of a quality suitable to the dignity, beauty, and history of the White House. Mrs. Kennedy's enthusiasm, supported by numerous friends, was responsible for establishing, in 1961, the White House Historical Association, a nonprofit organization "to enhance understanding, appreciation, and enjoyment of the Executive Mansion." But it is more than that. It is the official recipient of private, corporate, and foundation gifts for the purchase of objects for the White House, for its decoration and refurbishment and embellishment. And certainly no one was more successful than Mrs. Reagan in her efforts to attract funds for the association, or more skillful in their use. What she did, it seems quite apparent, was only the beginning. Certainly she wanted to give all Americans the opportunity of contributing to the beauty and continuity of the White House.

"When we arrived in January," Mrs. Reagan explained, "we looked into the warehouse where the furniture that is not in use is stored. We found beautiful pieces that were deteriorating and needed to be restored. Only a

BELOW LEFT: Mrs. Reagan and her daughter, Patricia, were the subjects of a portrait by Paul Clemens.

BELOW: The First Lady's Dressing Room was an inviting setting adjoining the First Family Bedroom on the second floor. Furniture included an 1830 tilt-top table and, at the foot of the bed, a small lacquered and gilded table with a Chinese porcelain plaque inlay.

The totally refurbished third floor was the "upstairs" of the first family's private quarters. It comprised a spacious Center Sitting Hall, surrounded by smaller sitting rooms and guest rooms. LEFT: To infuse the hall with warmth, architectural detailing and bookcases were given a *faux-bois* treatment, and the bookcases were also enhanced with trompe l'oeil pediments. Small conversation groupings encouraged informality; the one in the foreground included an early-nineteenth-century Sheraton sofa from Philadelphia, flanked by mahogany and satinwood card tables of the same era, from Boston.

very few pieces had to be purchased." She and the president declined to accept Congressional funds to refurbish their private quarters, but Mrs. Reagan soon received an immediate and generous reaction to her "special project"—an appeal for donations for this purpose. "I was overwhelmed by the response that came from people in all walks of life," she said. "Some of the contributions were for just one dollar." These donations were managed with great care. "Because funds were not available, some flooring had not been touched in many years," said Graber. "Plumbing and electrical wiring was obsolete; draperies were falling apart; there were mahogany doors that hadn't been attended to since President Truman's day." Upholstery was replaced and furniture restored, and a state dinner service—a complete one did not exist—was provided.

There were few details in which Mrs. Reagan herself did not take an interest. Even bibelots were important to her, for they are the things that make a home. "I can't really say I'm a collector," she explained, "but I do like to discover small objects—like those seals in the living room; I saw them in a shop in Spain." These were seals for wax, with handles of carnelian and onyx and mother-of-pearl and carved ivory. In the First Family Bedroom there was a collection of Battersea boxes on a table, and in the West Sitting Hall there were blue and white porcelains and jade objects. Everywhere there were personal touches. Among the many artworks displayed in the White House—for example, a Mary Cassatt in the Central Hall and a Cézanne in the West Sitting Hall—were two charming small paintings of beach scenes with women in nineteenth-century costumes. "One day when I was on my way to luncheon in Georgetown," said Mrs. Reagan, "I found them in an antiques shop next to the house where I was going."

One of the most extensive decorative changes Mrs. Reagan and Graber made in the private apartments was the transformation of the hall on the second floor. A wide, long expanse with Hoban's double-arched windows, like bouquets of light, at either end, it was a bare and awkward area until she and the designer filled the space properly. It became a sort of double drawing room, with an octagonal desk in the center, and comfortable furniture and screens on either side. The splendid proportions were still there, but the hall became, as Graber described it, "a place to walk about in and to sit and converse." A place, it must be added—like so much of the

newly decorated first family apartments—of elegance and easy charm.

Mrs. Reagan was justifiably pleased and proud. "Each room, when I look at it, seems to be my favorite," she said. "I feel we have accomplished what needed to be done, and I am very grateful to all those who have helped me in the project, not the least of whom are the members of the wonderful White House staff."

Graber was the first to attest to Mrs. Reagan's contributions to the result. "She has been deeply involved with everything we've done. She's given part of every day she's been in Washington to arranging the house exactly the way she thinks it should be." And the reason? "That's easy," said Mrs. Reagan with a smile. "This house belongs to all Americans, and I want it to be something of which they can be proud."

RIGHT: The First Family Bedroom, next to the President's Study on the second floor, had wallcovering handpainted in eighteenth-century style. Paintings included a landscape by Willard Metcalf, between the windows, and *Before Moonrise* by Carroll Sargent Tyson, on loan from the Philadelphia Museum of Art. The marble mantel was from an 1818 Washington, D.C., home designed by Benjamin Latrobe.

Catherine the Great's Chinese Jewel Box

Visiting a Rococo Conceit near St. Petersburg

Text by Peter Lauritzen
Photography by Lars Hansson

The very first building project of Catherine the Great's long reign involved a complex of small structures known as "Her Majesty's Own Dacha," built by the Italian-born architect Antonio Rinaldi on an estate some twenty-five miles southwest of St. Petersburg. The property had been laid out and developed in the second decade of the eighteenth century by Peter the Great's unscrupulous crony, Prince Alexander Menshikov. The palace that Menshikov built on a natural ridge overlooking the Gulf of Finland still exists, though in a terribly dilapidated and abandoned state. (Even before the revolution, the Baedeker guidebooks describe its interiors as being *"rien de particulier"*—nothing in particular.)

But the centerpiece of the royal dacha, the Chinese Palace, begun in 1762 and finished six years later, remains as a brilliant small jewel to delight visitors who are fortunate enough to find their way to it. From the outset, Menshikov's vast property was called Oranienbaum, following the German fashion affected by the courtiers of Peter the Great—the man who intended St. Petersburg to be Russia's first wholly European capital. Oranienbaum kept its German name until World War II. But after the terrible sufferings inflicted on St. Petersburg—then known as Leningrad—during the German army's long siege, a change was deemed appropriate, so in 1948 Oranienbaum became Lomonosov.

Ironically, Oranienbaum alone of all the great imperial summer residences was never occupied by the Nazi forces that virtually surrounded the city and kept it in a stranglehold from September 1941 to January 1944.

The Chinese Palace at Lomonosov—begun in 1762, the first year of Catherine the Great's reign—celebrates Rococo style. ABOVE: The spectacular Chinese Hall unites a dizzying array of elements: chinoiserie frescoes, Chinese and Japanese works of art, and a billiard table made in England. The architect, Antonio Rinaldi, designed the marquetry pictures fitted into the walls. The richly decorated ceiling is composed of Oriental fretwork, a small trompe-l'oeil dome, and a scalloped plasterwork frieze. OPPOSITE: The exterior hints at the lavish ornamentation within.

ABOVE: An oval anteroom
exemplifies the Rococo
palette of soft, pale colors.

ABOVE: The Hall of the Muses—identical in structure to the Chinese Hall at the opposite end of the palace—captures a decorative sensibility on the cusp of early Rococo. The wall paintings, 1768, are by Stefano Torelli of Bologna.

None of the buildings was looted or gutted, as were the better-known summer residences, such as nearby Peterhof (today Petrodvorets), Tsarskoye Selo (today Pushkin), and exquisite Pavlovsk—all of which stood as blackened, ravaged, and ruined shells of their former splendor after the German retreat. But neither has Lomonosov been besieged by the hordes of tourists who flock daily to see those other great monuments to Russia's imperial past and to the Soviet Union's determination and skill in creative reconstruction.

The village takes its modern name from the great Russian polymath, scientist, and man of letters Mikhail Vasilyevich Lomonosov, who during Catherine's reign founded a glass factory nearby. Ultimately, it was this local industry that made one of the most enchanting contributions to the Chinese Palace—and to eighteenth-

century interior decoration—in the form of the palace's beaded room.

The edifice itself was hardly a palace on the scale that Catherine's predecessor, the empress Elizabeth, would have recognized. Indeed, its relatively restrained exterior stood two stories high, and the building contained just seventeen rooms. But at least three of these are among the most pleasing survivors from Catherine's reign, and all the more extraordinary for having come through World War II unharmed.

Only one large room of the palace is decorated in the fashionable chinoiserie style that gives the building as a whole its name. There, the ceiling is a riot of Rococo plasterwork cartouches and gilt fronds framing Chinese patterns and geometrical motifs, while the walls and floors are a tour de force of intarsia work. Costumed figures and Oriental landscapes are set into the walls against a backdrop of natural, unvarnished wood grain. This remarkable room is furnished with blue-and-white Chinese vases, black japanned chests, and European chinoiserie chairs. Today, an immense eighteenth-century billiard table—with handsome carved paw feet proclaiming its English origins—stands somewhat incongruously in the center of the room.

The corresponding hall at the far end of the building reflects the other end of eighteenth-century taste in interior decoration, with pale *faux-marbre* walls divided into more restful classical shapes. This delightful sunny room, open to the park on both sides and finished with graceful paintings representing the nine Muses by Italian artist Stefano Torelli, is a European counterpart to the exotica of the Chinese chamber.

Midway between these two spaces stands a smaller room whose walls are lined with what at first appear to be beautiful embroidered-silk panels. However, these panels glisten with an unusually intense sheen that arrests the visitor's glance and arouses immediate curiosity. On closer inspection, their brilliant ground reveals itself to be not woven silk but a mosaic of minute glass beads, created especially for the room in Lomonosov's glassworks.

The empress was suitably proud of this exquisite jewel box, and in subsequent years members of the diplomatic corps were often brought to Oranienbaum to admire the Chinese Palace and its lavish décor. But delighted as Catherine may have been with the achievement, on the whole she hardly used her Chinese Palace at all. The empress had many other projects to absorb her time and attention, and follies such as this one were like her lovers, never intended as more than a temporary divertissement to satisfy a royal whim.

A Mongolian Yurt

Continuing the Ancient Tradition of Movable Homes

Text and Photography by Herman How-Man Wong

A visitor to Inner Mongolia is at once arrested by the view—a vast expanse of silent land, an unbroken horizon. The arid steppe is punctuated by occasional stretches of green, while subdued sunlight—it is quite far north—discloses small clusters of pale domed shapes that blend with the landscape. Closer inspection reveals movement. Human and animal activity indicates a community: The round structures are Mongol homes.

The yurt, or *ger*, as it is more commonly known in central Asia, is a felt tent that has served as the basic dwelling for the inhabitants of that region for centuries. Its greatest asset is flexibility, accommodating the nomadic life of people who must move with their animals—sheep, goats, cattle, camels—in search of fresh grazing grounds. Easily collapsible and transportable, a yurt can be raised by two persons in as little as half an hour, and disassembled and put away in the same amount of time.

Structurally, a yurt is a circular tent with an expandable frame, twenty to thirty feet in diameter. The frame consists of four to twelve lattice base walls, or *khanas*, depending on the size and wealth of the family. It is said,

though this is not necessarily the case, that a *khana* is added for each new family member and his or her furniture and belongings.

A yurt is assembled in a specific order. First, all large furniture pieces are placed in what will be the interior—later the walls will be built around them. The collapsible wood floor, or matt, is then laid; the four-foot-high lattice walls, and the door, facing south, are set around it. When the dome framework is raised, the structure resembles the skeleton of a vast umbrella. The entire frame is then covered with several layers of heavy felt, usually made of yak or sheep wool, held in place by three ropes. The opening in the top functions as a skylight and allows for the passage of smoke and cooking fumes.

The yurt is a wonderful example of indigenous architecture—and human resourcefulness. Throughout the world, generation after generation has experimented to find the very best sizes, shapes, and locations for their dwellings. By using available natural materials, and without sophisticated tools or machinery, they have constructed houses that conform to and enhance their way

Though modern technology has begun to influence the nomads of lower Mongolia, these descendants of Genghis Khan steadfastly adhere to their traditional way of life. They continue to live in yurts—structures covered with layers of felt made from yak or sheep wool—which offer protection from climatic extremes. OPPOSITE: Domed yurts are specks on the vast steppe of Inner Mongolia. Red doors softly reflect the last vestiges of daylight.

LEFT: Despite its small size, the Mongolian horse is swift and powerful. The pole with a lasso is used to catch horses in stampede.

RIGHT: A young Mongolian
girl in native dress stands
beside her home. The small
door allows a minimum of
heat to escape when open,
while mortar packed against
the base prevents drafts
and stops rainwater from
leaking in.

of life. In some cultures a house must provide areas for cooking, for sleeping, for privacy, and for social gatherings and entertainment. It must have adequate storage and room for belongings. In others, a "house" may be nothing more than straw matting propped up to break the wind, providing a place to sleep. Whatever the requirements, as a refuge it must exist in harmony with the climate. Mediterranean houses can be opened to welcome sea breezes, and shut tight against the searing afternoon sun. Those in Southeast Asia must, of necessity, rise above the floodwaters of the monsoons. Alpine homes have steeply pitched roofs to shed snow. The rounded yurt is ideally suited to life on the steppes of Inner Mongolia.

Capable of maintaining comfortably warm temperatures in the harsh winters, the yurt is similarly adaptable to summer weather, when it is covered with a lighter material and waterproof canvas. In extreme heat, the lower section of the coverings is rolled up, leaving the lattice walls exposed, to provide substantial ventilation. The flexible framework also is earthquake resistant.

Modern technology is beginning to affect the Mongols. More scientific use of the land has enabled them to remain in one place for longer periods of time. Generators provide them with electric power. Even the tedious work of acquiring materials for their homes is seldom necessary today; prefabricated yurts can now be purchased. However, although science may simplify some of the rigors of their existence, these people have no desire to relinquish their way of life in favor of a sedentary existence—or to abandon their historic tradition of nomadism.

ABOVE: A yurt, belonging to an affluent family and reserved solely for entertaining, has floors covered with thick rugs and lattice walls lined with brightly patterned fabric.

ABOVE: The Chinese influence is evident in the door, which is decorated with traditional patterns. A scarcity of wood on the steppe makes all such objects valued family possessions.

RIGHT: Like the ribs of a huge umbrella, the supporting poles form the domed roof. The vent can be controlled, functioning as a smoke outlet for the stove and its collapsible chimney as well as a skylight. Large furniture is placed around the periphery, giving a feeling of spaciousness to the interior.

St. Croix Pyramids

Geometries Define a House
in the U.S. Virgin Islands

Architecture by Donald C. Smith, AIA
Interior Design by Carol A. Groh, ASID
Text by Steven M. L. Aronson
Photography by Dan Forer

Unlike fair-weather friends, friends of fair weather will
go to great lengths. When Donald C. Smith, former
chairman of the huge architectural firm of Skidmore,
Owings & Merrill, and his wife, Carol A. Groh, a seasoned designer of commercial interiors, were looking to
build a vacation house in a place where the climate was
always clement, they did some research and headed for
the U.S. Virgin Islands, with its year-round temperature
spread of only seven degrees. They had a good look at St.
John ("most of it was a national park") and St. Thomas
("too built up") and then, their dreams dampened, took
the next flight out. But as their plane passed over the
third U.S. Virgin, St. Croix, Smith happened to glance
out the window.

"There was a land mass jutting out with nothing on
it," recalls Groh, "and Don yelled, 'Sam'—which is what
he calls me—'that's it, that's for us!'" Two weeks later
they not only owned thirteen acres of the area they'd
previewed from the window but had already earmarked
the best site to build their house on. Then six months
down the road, with the design work all but done, Smith

RIGHT: Seven pyramidal
structures and glazed walls
shape the house that Donald
C. Smith, former chairman
of Skidmore, Owings &
Merrill, and his wife, interior
designer Carol A. Groh, built
on St. Croix. Twilight reveals
the transparent nature of
the residence.

ABOVE: A grouping of native stones "serves as a focal point when one approaches the house," says Smith. "I like the rhythm of the rugged stone against the sleek pyramids."

RIGHT: "In this house it's like living on a boat," says Groh. "You're right out in the middle of the water." Situated on the peninsula of Anna's Hope, the house has 270 degrees of water views. "At night the stars and the twinkling lights of Christiansted are unbelievable," adds Smith.

came home one day to the island house they were renting and said to his wife, "Hold everything—I just found a better property."

They got in the jeep and drove three miles to a four-acre peninsula and bought that, too. It was higher off the sea (therefore more protected as well as more dramatic), and it also happened to form the eastern end of the island's most beautiful beach. They chose a site clear out on the point, and Smith, an architect who had built bank buildings, office towers, apartment houses, and award-winning galleries but never a residential house, went to work adapting his original design.

"For both of us, the pyramid was the most beautiful architectural proportion—we'd been to Egypt many times—and here it seemed exactly the right form," he explains. Today the house is known from one end of the island to the other as the Pyramid House. "Actually, it's everybody else who calls it that—I call it," Smith laughs, "the Smith House, and my wife calls it the Groh House."

Smith and Groh sounded their architectural intentions right at the front gate, making it a pyramid twenty feet high. Beyond, a long palm-lined driveway ends in a circle that marks the beginning of the granite path up to the house. To the left of this walkway is a twenty-five-foot-high structure made of local bluestone (as a nod to custom, the couple took care to build three small versions of the sugar mills indigenous to the island; two of them house mechanical equipment, and the third, situated on the path to the beach, functions as a changing room and shower). Thanks to abundant planting, you catch only

"I can't stand a dark room," says Smith. ABOVE: The view from the entrance hall takes in the garden court, with its lush foliage, the dining room and the ocean beyond. A glass pyramid roof lets the sun in. "All the other rooms—and even the closets—have skylights."

fugitive glimpses of sea along the walk. But just a few steps inside the front door you encounter a glass-enclosed garden court and suddenly the whole place is awash in the clear light of the ocean.

The house was ingeniously conceived as seven major spaces—a living room twenty-four feet square and six additional rooms eighteen feet square, each of them ending in a twenty-five-foot-high pyramidal peak. While the pyramid in the garden court is all glass to allow ample light for plants, the other pyramids are mostly solid wood (light-colored mahogany imported from Africa), becoming glass only for a last few skylit feet. "I felt that a room deserved to have more than just flat space," says Smith. "I wanted these rooms to breathe and to soar." Every pyramid is supported by four concrete columns (painted stark white—"the right color for the islands") and lit from its base to give a full sense of the structure of the architecture.

For Groh, the most important single element in the house was the floor. If the concept was always to use it to bring the outside and inside together, the question remained how. "I kept studying the color of the ocean and how the light played on it, and I decided I needed marble," she says. "It carries the feel of the sea right into the house." There's a soft green sheen to the Chinese marble she selected for every square foot of flooring in all the rooms and on all the terraces. "And it's also cool to walk on and easy to maintain."

There are no solid walls—just sliding glass doors—in the entertainment wing, which consists of living room, dining room, kitchen and the glazed garden court. As for that bright central space, being a true garden it has a path (albeit an indoor one), not to mention tropical plants, sago palms and a twenty-foot-high pandanus tree that create density and foreground. There's no furniture here, unless you count the three boulders brought in by tractor.

The garden court is separated on the right from the kitchen and on the left from the living room by handsome white-painted floor-to-ceiling grid screens. "You

RIGHT: Mullioned window walls in the main rooms slide in from the corners so that "the house breathes from all directions."

can see through them, yet at the same time you have some definition of space," says Groh. Smith adds, "I wanted the house to be transparent but I also wanted it to have some mystery—to me, those grid screens are like architectural negligees." The only place there they wound up not putting a grid is between the garden court and the dining room—in order to preserve the panorama of sea.

In the living room, views of Christiansted three miles away loom large and bright—midday is never pale here. Wicker, because it's light, airy and open, was chosen for sofas, club chairs and ottomans; cushions were covered in simple white cotton chenille, and pillows were made up in bougainvillea colors. Groh designed a big square low table with glazed polyester sides, spray-painted it a greenish sea color, lit it from within, and floated it off the floor. "I always knew that when we built our house in the

islands," she confides, "I would furnish it as minimally as possible." The living room is girded by three terraces; the one to the west looks out on a cerulean-blue-tiled swimming pool, perfectly round. The land then drops forty feet to the sea, exposing craggy rocks covered with spiky monkey trees.

The couple positioned the dining room as far out on the point as they could get it, angling it north toward St. John and St. Thomas, and the ineluctable effect is of supping mid-sea. Terraces hug the room on two sides, east and west. The dining table is a dark green slab of oceanic marble landlocked by a pedestal of white-painted wood; in the center Groh implanted a piece of glass talismanically etched with a pyramid. The bentwood maple dining chairs were designed by Davis Allen, former head of interiors at Skidmore, Owings & Merrill.

ABOVE: White-painted concrete beams support the African mahogany pyramid ceiling in the dining room. The triangular arrangement of beams "adds interest and makes for a stronger structure," Smith says. Groh designed the marble-top table with a lighted glass inset.

From the main body of the house you have to step out onto a walkway to get to the bedrooms in the back—three separate enclosures all contained under the same roof frame as the rest of the house. Sweeping simplicity is the note struck here: king-size beds, Egyptian cotton coverlets, wicker chairs and ottomans, and cotton pillows in fuchsia, purple, and pink. Each bedroom comes equipped with a sunset-friendly terrace to the west.

Soft air flows through the house leeward and windward; outside, the sea is the green of peace and the blue of rumination. Not surprisingly, the pleasure pyramid that the Smiths built as a "getaway house" has over the years become their main residence. "By the time the pharaohs got to their pyramids, they were dead," says Donald Smith. "We built our pyramid so we could live in paradise."

ABOVE AND LEFT: "I've always got to be out looking for the sun, celebrating it," says Smith. The western terrace off the living room is laid with Chinese marble ("The way it reflects light is just like the sea") and features a round swimming pool.

Pacific Overture

A Malibu Home Moves the Outside In

Architecture by John Lautner
Interior Design by Michael Taylor
Text by Jesse Kornbluth
Photography by Russell MacMasters

When Michael Taylor was a young man, he worked on the interior of a Frank Lloyd Wright house in California. It was a difficult, unique, and satisfying job, and it convinced him, at age twenty-one, that it was more sensible to scale home furnishings to the architecture around them than to focus on filling rooms with beautiful pieces.

Over the years, Taylor successfully tested this conviction in spaces so diverse that it is hard to cite a category he's missed. He designed villas in Arizona and houses in Saudi Arabia. He did executive offices in Philip Johnson buildings. He outfitted ships and decorated planes.

But when longtime clients in Los Angeles asked him to help build a dream house, Taylor knew he was in for a different challenge. The clients were a businessman and his wife, people whose acumen was matched only by their stamina and taste. And the land they had selected for the house called for a design as extraordinary as its setting—a large lot so far out on a rocky point in Malibu that it was practically in the ocean.

The designer suggested that the ideal architect for this house would be John Lautner, a veteran Los Angeles architect whose work, like Taylor's, emphasizes originality and appropriateness. Together, they came up with a design that brought the point literally inside the house. By building the house around boulders and continuing that theme with slate flooring, they would give the owners a harmony with nature that many aspire to but few ever achieve.

Thirteen years and five plans later, Taylor and supervising architect Richard Turner completed a dwelling that Taylor ranked among the best he'd ever done. Far from exhausting him, the experience was exhilarating.

Confronted with such a wild and barren site, lesser talents might have emphasized the building's architectural and structural originality at the expense of its vistas. But the team in place made the house—a large, free-flowing space with a high sloping ceiling and window walls—a kind of observation deck. Beyond the interior

In keeping with the owners' wish to live in harmony with nature, designer Michael Taylor and architect John Lautner used rock extensively throughout a Malibu residence situated on a rugged promontory. The results elicited just one complaint from the businessman husband: "Now I resent having to leave home." OPPOSITE: An antique Chinese table adds an exotic patina to the slate-floored entrance hall, dominated by a riverbed boulder. The loft hovers above.

FAR LEFT: The successful melding of exterior and interior spaces is evident in the materials—rock and slate—used in the garden courtyard, which was conceived by Taylor.

LEFT: Expansive ocean vistas and exterior stainless-steel railings lend a shipboard mood to the window-walled living area, where even the floor seems to glisten with a watery luster. A Shiva lingham tops an angular table, embellishing one of the several conversation groupings that punctuate the flowing space.

ABOVE: A boulder serves
as a hearth in the master
bedroom.

boulders and man-made treasures was the rarest of back-yards: an essentially private beach, a cove where spearfish-ers dove for bass, and a coastline so deserted that there were only five houses on a ten-mile stretch of sand.

In the setting, just as Taylor predicted, the indoor rocks did not dominate but enhance. This was a considerable achievement, for these weren't just any stones—they were enormous boulders, one weighing more than twenty tons. The clients, Turner, and Taylor waded in riverbeds hun-dreds of miles from Malibu to find them. Roadways were bulldozed to give a hydro-crane access to the riverbed. Spe-cial nylon slings were ordered to prevent damage to the rocks on the seven-hour trip south. And finally the rocks were steam-cleaned and sealed to prevent fungal growth.

With the riverbed boulders set in Malibu sand, con-struction finally began. Like everything else about this project, it was not commonplace. While the ninety-foot single-span roof was being erected, Taylor and Turner were laying out thick slabs of slate on the beach, sawing

them up to make a "free-form carpet," then hauling the pieces into the house for final assembly. Later, special glass cutters were hired to fit half-inch-thick glass walls into the rocks. Other specialists were called in to carve sinks out of the slabs of solid granite in the baths.

And that was largely it.

"When you have a fabulous view," Taylor said, "you want every inch of it. That means no carpets, no draperies, no upholstered furniture." And no pastels or soothing woods, either: "You'd think you'd want wood, on that severe point, to keep the rooms from being cold, but in this case repeating the outside elements does that just as well."

Taylor designed the appropriately proportioned chairs and granite-and-glass lamps. He set the clients' extraordinary collection of Pre-Columbian and New Guinea artifacts on concrete shelves. And then he selected a piece of "real" furniture—an antique Chinese table that in this setting looks almost contemporary. The clients installed their Bösendorfer piano and a cherished

BELOW: A sitting area, just steps above the living area, displays the clients' collection of Pre-Columbian figures.

manuscript page of Beethoven's *Piano Concerto No. 5*, and moved in. Their one regret: The home's acoustics weren't good for the piano.

Art? The walls were purposefully bare. "I've always suggested blank walls when you can't find the perfect thing," the designer said. "Then you have a wall for dreaming, for relief. But here the situation is different. The rocks, the floors, and the view are art enough. And when the clients are there, they take over—adding their own quality of warmth."

Contributors

Jaime Ardiles-Arce is a photographer and frequent contributor to *Architectural Digest*. He divides his time between Greece, Paris, and New York.

Steven M. L. Aronson is a contributing writer for *Architectural Digest*. He is the author of *Hype* and the coauthor of *Savage Grace*. A former book editor and publisher, he is currently writing *Class Act: The Life of Leland Hayward*.

Harry Benson is a photographer whose books include *Harry Benson: 50 Years in Pictures*, *Harry Benson's America*, and *Tivoli Gardens*.

Christopher Buckley is the author of numerous books, including *Thank You for Smoking*, *No Way to Treat a First Lady*, and, most recently, *Boomsday*.

Sam Burchell was a senior editor for *Architectural Digest*.

John A. Cherol is a writer and former curator and executive director of the Preservation Society of Newport County.

Richard Corman is a photographer based in New York.

Stephen Drucker, a former contributing writer to *Architectural Digest*, is editor in chief of *House Beautiful*.

Marina Faust is a contributing photographer to *Architectural Digest*. She is based in Paris and coauthored, with Dana Micucci, *Artists in Residence: A Guide to the Homes and Studios of Eight Nineteenth-Century Painters In and Around Paris*.

Dan Forer is a contributing photographer to *Architectural Digest*. He is based in Miami and has been a photographer of architecture and interior design for more than thirty years.

Scott Frances is a contributing photographer to *Architectural Digest*. He is based in New York.

Elizabeth Gaynor is an author whose books include *Finland Living Design* and—in collaboration with author Kari Haavisto—*Stylish Solutions* and *Russian Houses*.

Joseph Giovannini is a contributing writer to *Architectural Digest*. He is a practicing architect and author of *Materializing the Immaterial: The Architecture of Wallace Cunningham*.

Kari Haavisto is an author whose books include *Stylish Solutions* and *Russian Houses*, both coauthored with Elizabeth Gaynor.

Steve Hall is a partner at the Chicago photography firm Hedrich Blessing.

Lars Hansson is a photographer based in Stockholm, Sweden.

Verlyn Klinkenborg, a former contributing writer to *Architectural Digest*, is a member of *The New York Times* editorial board. His books include *The Rural Life* and *Timothy, or Notes of an Abject Reptile*.

Jesse Kornbluth is a New York–based writer and the founder and editor of HeadButler.com.

Elizabeth Lambert is a writer and frequent contributor to *Architectural Digest*. She is based in London.

Peter Lauritzen is a writer and historian whose books include *Venice: A Thousand Years of Culture and Civilization* and *Rome: Mirror of the Centuries*.

Massimo Listri is a photographer based in Florence. His work has appeared in *Villas of Tuscany* and *Magnificent Italian Villas and Palaces*.

Carol Lutfy is a writer whose specialty is Asian design and architecture.

Russell Lynes was the president of the Archives of American Art and a columnist for *Art in America*. He published numerous books and articles, primarily on American taste and manners, and was a founding member of the Landmarks Preservation Commission of New York.

Russell MacMasters is a former photographer for *Architectural Digest*.

Philip Mansel is a historian and biographer whose books include *Dressed to Rule: Royal and Court Costume from Louis XIV to Elizabeth II* and *Sultans in Splendor: Monarchs of the Middle East 1869–1945*. He is a cofounder of the Society for Court Studies and divides his time between London and Istanbul.

David O. Marlow is a contributing photographer to *Architectural Digest*. He is based in Aspen, Colorado.

Dana Micucci is a New York–based writer. Her books include *Best Bids: The Insider's Guide to Buying at Auction* and *Artists in Residence: A Guide to the Homes and Studios of Eight Nineteenth-Century Artists In and Around Paris*.

Derry Moore is a contributing photographer to *Architectural Digest* whose photographs have appeared in several books including *Notting Hill*, *A Gardener's Life*, and, most recently, *Rooms*.

Mary E. Nichols is a contributing photographer to *Architectural Digest*. Her photographs have appeared in numerous books, including *Blair House: The President's Guesthouse*. She is based in Los Angeles.

Brooks Peters was a writer and editor for several American design publications and former editor in chief of *Quest Magazine*. He now runs an antiquarian bookstore, Brooks Books, and is at work on a family memoir.

Erhard Pfeiffer is a contributing photographer to *Architectural Digest*. His photographs of architecture, interior design, hotels, and residences have appeared in numerous books and publications worldwide. He is based in Los Angeles but covers assignments in the United States as well as Asia, Europe, and South America.

Jonathan Pilkington is a photographer and a frequent contributor to *Architectural Digest*. He is based in London.

Prince Michael of Greece is a writer and historian whose books include *Jewels of the Tsars*, *Imperial Palaces of Russia*, and, most recently, *Le Rajah de Bourbon*.

Robert Reck is a contributing photographer to *Architectural Digest*. His most recent books are *The Small Adobe House* and *Facing Southwest: The Life and Houses of John Gaw Meem*. He is based in Albuquerque, New Mexico.

Durston Saylor is a contributing photographer to *Architectural Digest* whose photos have appeared in more than thirty books on architecture and interior design. He is based in New York.

Tony Soluri is a contributing photographer to *Architectural Digest*. He is based in Chicago.

Tim Street-Porter is a contributing photographer to *Architectural Digest* and is the author of *Los Angeles*, *Tropical Houses*, *Freestyle*, and *Casa Mexicana*. He is based in Los Angeles.

Judith Thurman is a contributing writer to *Architectural Digest*. She is the author of the biographies *Isak Dinesen: The Life of a Storyteller*, which won a National Book Award, and *Secrets of the Flesh: A Life of Colette*. She writes regularly for *The New Yorker*.

Jeff Turrentine is a contributing writer to *Architectural Digest* and a former staff writer for *The Washington Post*. His articles have appeared in a variety of publications, such as *The New York Times* and *The Los Angeles Times*.

Andrew Twort is a photographer and a frequent contributor to *Architectural Digest*. He is based in the United Kingdom.

Pilar Viladas is the design editor of *The New York Times Magazine*. Her books include *Domesticities: At Home with The New York Times Magazine* and *California Beach Houses: Style, Interiors, and Architecture*.

Paul Warchol is a photographer and frequent contributor to *Architectural Digest*. He has been photographing architecture since 1978 and has been featured in architectural publications worldwide.

Michael Webb is the author of such books as *Modernism Reborn: Midcentury American Houses* and *Venice, CA: Art and Architecture in a Maverick Community*.

Herman How-Man Wong is a writer who has explored China's remote regions and documented their disappearing cultures.

Sally Woodbridge is an architectural historian and the editor and author of numerous books on architecture.

Photography Credits

The Czar's Private Apartments in the Kremlin (appeared in May 1992 issue): pages 8–15 by Jaime Ardiles-Arce and Yuri Dimitriev

Georgia O'Keeffe's Ghost Ranch (March 2002): page 17 by Mary E. Nichols; pages 16, 18–23 by Robert Reck

David Bowie (September 1992): pages 24–31 by Derry Moore

John Loring's Red House (July 1993): pages 32–37 by Tony Soluri

Crow Hollow Ranch (September 1996): pages 38–43 by David O. Marlow

New Life for the Château du Marais (September 2006): pages 44–49 by Marina Faust

Sculptural Fantasy (August 1992): pages 50–57 by Jaime Ardiles-Arce

Changing Seasons in Kyoto (May 1993): pages 58–63 by Jaime Ardiles-Arce

Wyntoon (January 1888 and December 2002): pages 64–69 by Tim Street-Porter

Ohio Organic (March 2001): pages 70–77 by Scott Frances

Between a Rock and a Hard Place in Utah (June 1993): pages 78–83 by Mary E. Nichols

New York Primaries (August 1997): pages 84–91 by Paul Warchol

Ralph Lauren's Bedford Beauty (November 2004): page 100 (left) by Richard Corman; pages 92–101 by Durston Saylor

Gilded Age Glory (October 1985): pages 102–107 by Derry Moore

Glass Geometries (May 1995): pages 108–115 by Jaime Ardiles-Arce

Evolution in Los Angeles (September 1996): pages 116–121 by Mary E. Nichols

House of Cards (September 1987): pages 122–127 by Massimo Listri

Spinning the Senses (December 2002): pages 128–135 by Erhard Pfeiffer

Ole Bull's Little Alhambra (December 1992): pages 136–143 by Kari Haavisto

Giorgio Armani (November 2006): page 147 (above) by Harry Benson; pages 144–150 by Durston Saylor

Haga Pavilion (October 1990): pages 152–159 by José Luis Pérez

A Kenyan Sanctuary (September 1995): pages 160–165 by Jonathan Pilkington

Pride and Preservation (January 2005): pages 166–173 by Andrew Twort

Out of the Blue (June 2007): pages 174–179 by Steve Hall/Hedrich Blessing

Tropical Infusion (July 2004): pages 180–185 by Scott Frances

President and Mrs. Ronald Reagan's White House (December 1981 and December 2004): pages 186–193 by Derry Moore

Catherine the Great's Chinese Jewel Box (October 1989): pages 194–199 by Lars Hansson

A Mongolian Yurt (July 1982): pages 200–203 by Herman How-Man Wong

St. Croix Pyramids (January 1998): pages 204–211 by Dan Forer

Pacific Overture (May 1985): pages 212–217 by Russell MacMasters

Index

Page numbers in *italics* refer to photographs.